The *Marco Polo* painted by Thomas Robertson, 1859

The Wind And The Sails

The Wind And The Sails

The story of the Marco Polo and the Canadians who transformed the shipping world

Peter W Noonan

MAGISTRALIS

Ottawa, Canada

The Wind And The Sails Copyright © 2025 by Peter W Noonan. All Rights Reserved

ISBN: 978-1-7780030-8-0 (Paperback)

ISBN: 978-1-7780030-9-7 (E-Book)

For Cataloguing in Publication Data refer to:

Library and Archives Canada
395 Wellington St, Ottawa, ON K1A 0J1
Canada

Contents

The Vanished Era of the Great Wind Ships   1

PART I. MAIN BODY

1. Chapter 1. Donald McKay and the Evolution of the Clipper Ship   *3*
2. Chapter 2. Samuel Cunard and the Rise of the Steamship   *21*
3. Chapter 3. James Smith and the Marco Polo   *32*
4. Chapter 4. A Botched Launching and a Maiden Voyage   *40*
5. Chapter 5. Enter James Baines   *47*
6. Chapter 6. The Fastest Ship in the World   *54*
7. Chapter 7. Fifteen Thousand Australians   *66*
8. Chapter 8. Steam Catches Sail   *74*
9. Chapter 9. The Final Years   *88*

Epilogue: Remembrance   *95*
Appendix: Who was Marco Polo?   *100*
Image Credits   *104*
Bibliography   *106*

The Wind And The Sails

The Vanished Era of the Great Wind Ships

For hundreds of years, humans propelled themselves across the oceans by harnessing the power of the wind. Over the centuries ship designers perfected their craft until, ultimately, in the nineteenth century, the design of wind ships reached their zenith in the great transoceanic clipper ships. With their towering masts and billowing sails reaching far skyward the clipper ships were the fastest sailing ships and most beautiful sea craft, that have ever graced the oceans. And yet the triumph of the clipper ship was only ephemeral. A quarter of a century after their emergence they had largely disappeared from the seas. In their place, the ungainly steamship with its billowing black smoke replaced the forests of masts and the clouds of white sails of the evanescent clippers.

In the drama on the high seas that saw the rise of the greatest of all the wind ships, and their subsequent fall to the power of steam, two Canadians played transformational roles. Donald McKay, a master shipbuilder from Nova Scotia, designed and built the greatest of all the clipper ships for both American and British shipowners, and Samuel Cunard, a shipowner, and merchant from Nova Scotia, was a pivotal figure in the ultimate triumph of steam power on the world's oceans. A third Canadian, James Smith of New Brunswick would design and build the fabulous Canadian clipper *Marco Polo*, once the most famous ship on the oceans.

This is the story of a great ship in the romantic era of the classic wind ships, and the story of Canadians who fostered the rise of the clippers and heralded their ultimate demise with the technological triumph of steam power at the end of the nineteenth century.

1

Chapter 1. Donald McKay and the Evolution of the Clipper Ship

At the beginning of the nineteenth century, the world was still a vast place and travel and communications between the hemispheres often took many months aboard slow merchant ships. Shipbuilding technology had made only limited progress in the preceding centuries, especially in connection with merchant ships. The standard merchant vessel of the early nineteenth century was the East Indiamen or some version of it. The East Indiamen were named after Great Britain's East India Company, the monopoly that ruled British India at the start of the nineteenth century. In general terms, an East Indiaman was usually 175 feet long and 30 feet wide, bluff-bowed with a rounded hull and a deep draught. They were slow, but they provided ample cargo capacity. These slow merchantmen followed Admiralty-prescribed routes to the Far East and took many months to accomplish a voyage. Because Britain's Navigation Laws prevented foreign ships from competing with them for British cargoes there was little incentive for shipbuilders in the British Empire to try to advance the shipbuilding technology beyond the existing conventional design.

But change was coming. The bold new United States of America had broken with Europe in the last decades of the eighteenth century and its traders were imbued with a spirit of competition. American shipowners and shipbuilders perceived that profits could be made by producing speedy ships for international trade. Therefore, they began to craft vessels that could speedily deliver cargoes to and from American and foreign ports and outrun, and outmaneuvre, marauding vessels from foreign countries. Thus began a great technological evolution of the sailing ship that would change world markets and public perceptions about the time needed to travel or communicate with far-off places. The world would soon begin to seem smaller owing to the development of the clipper ship.

Few things upon the seas were as beautiful to behold as the great clipper ships of the nineteenth century. They evolved first in America, where the quest for speed was highly valued. In pre-revolutionary America smuggling was rampant and a fast ship was essential for those who sought to outwit the revenue cutters of the British administration. Later, the merchant ships of the new United States of America would fall prey to the depredations of the pirates of Tripolitania, and to the privateers and naval vessels of both France and Britain. In the absence of a strong American navy American shipping firms placed a premium on ships that could outrun any pursuer.

American shipbuilders located around Chesapeake Bay began looking to France for inspiration, and to the beautiful fast frigates that were built for the French navy. The result, in the early nineteenth century, was the development of the Virginia Pilot Boat and then the very fast Baltimore Clipper, a type of ship that was influenced both by French designs and by the Bermuda Sloop. These small fast ships were named after Baltimore, the major city located on Chesapeake Bay. They were topsail schooners or brigantines, with raked masts and sharp bows and sterns, and their sterns lay deeper in the water than the bows of the ship. Their swept-back rakish bows and sharp sterns provided them with a deck that exceeded the length of their keels. And their hull design resembled a V rather than the traditional U shape that characterized most merchant vessels, with a draught that increased towards the stern of the vessel. Baltimore Clippers also had a lower freeboard than was typical for ship designs of those times and their masts were quite noticeably canted towards the stern. Most of their width was placed forward, like their French precursors. The result was a combination of beauty and speed.

Baltimore Clippers proved to be particularly useful to America during the War of 1812, between the United States and the British Empire. During that war, the US employed Baltimore Clippers as privateers to challenge British shipping. However, after the war, American shipbuilders responded to market demands for slower and fatter merchant ships that could carry larger cargoes. However, American ship designers did not forget the utility of speed, nor did the Baltimore Clippers disappear. After the war fast ships, such as the Baltimore Clippers, could still be found in niche trades such as smuggling, opium carriers, and among slave ships (and also sometimes as US government revenue cutters).

From time to time designers were able to craft a ship for speed based on the principles they had learned from building the earlier ships. Perhaps the most notable of such ships designed and constructed in America as the century progressed was the *Ann McKim*, often said to be a forerunner of the true clipper ship. Built in 1832 she had a hull that was similar to a Baltimore Clipper but unlike the Baltimore Clippers, the *Ann McKim* was a square-rigger, rather than a topsail schooner. She developed a reputation for speed that was gained over a 20-year career carrying cargoes to and from the USA to South America, and also to and from China.

Meanwhile, in Canada, in Nova Scotia, a boy was reaching manhood who would establish the evolving clipper ship as the height of grace and beauty upon the high seas. His name was Donald McKay and he was born on September 4, 1810, in Jordan Falls, Shelburne County, Nova Scotia, to a Scottish-Canadian farmer and his wife. From his boyhood, Donald

The Wind And The Sails

McKay was smitten by the sea and ships despite his family's agricultural roots. Although shipbuilding was a substantial activity in Nova Scotia most of the shipbuilding activity was centred in and around the provincial capital of Halifax, and there was relatively less shipbuilding in the south of the province where Shelburne lay. However, in Shelburne there was a local shipbuilder named McIntire and, in 1824, a thirteen-year-old Donald McKay, intent on pursuing his dream of becoming a shipbuilder, secured employment at McIntire's shipyard in Shelburne. Most of McIntire's work consisted of ship repair or the construction of fishing dories for which there was a constant demand because fishing, along with agriculture, were two of the most important industries in and around Shelburne.

In Shelburne, McKay watched and learned the craft of boatbuilding through the use of the two-man saw, sanding down boat keels, applying caulking to boat planking with ravelled rope, painting the dories, splicing rope, and mending sails. The following year Donald and his brother Lachlan decided to try to build a boat on their own. Taking a spot adjacent to the McIntire yard they worked on their project whenever they could. Donald McKay's kindly master kept an eye on their progress and when the two brothers finished their boat in 1826, he pronounced it to be a very satisfactory dory. The boat was finished with a mast and sail and it was deemed good enough to be purchased by a local fisherman.

By now Donald McKay's ambition drove him to look farther

afield and when a coaster stopped in Shelburne for repairs and he learned that it was New York bound he signed on as a crewman for the voyage south knowing that New York was the major shipbuilding centre in eastern North America. When McKay arrived in New York in the fall of 1826, he would, no doubt, have been immediately overwhelmed by the sight of that bustling commercial metropolis with its five-story warehouses and its harbour filled with ships coming and going to and from ports all over the world. That same year the Erie Canal had been completed and the east coast shipping business was booming as new markets opened around the Great Lakes and in the Old Northwest. So there was plenty of work and McKay soon found employment in the shipyard of Isaac Webb, where he entered into articles of apprenticeship and served his master from the age of sixteen to the age of twenty-one. In his apprenticeship contract, McKay had to pledge "not to play at cards or dice, haunt alehouses, taverns, dance houses or play houses."[1]

The New York shipyards were the most technologically advanced in North America during this period, which was amply demonstrated by their use of steam derricks, and steam or water-powered saws and lathes. At Isaac Webb's shipyard, McKay was exposed to the full range of shipbuilding techniques and artisanal knowledge including the setting of the keel, the attachment of the curved ribs to the keel, the installation of crossbeams using treenails, the planking of a framed ship, and the caulking of a planked hull with oakum and ravelled hemp for waterproofing. Only when the hull was completed were the deck planks installed and then finally the fittings (hatches, rails, etc.) were put in just before the hull was launched.

After leaving the Isaac Webb shipyard at the end of his apprenticeship McKay briefly returned to Nova Scotia where he built a ship in partnership with an uncle but it proved to be financially unsuccessful.[2] McKay then returned to New York and joined the Brown and Bell shipyard as a journeyman shipwright. During his time with that yard, McKay also met and married Albenia Boole, a fellow Nova Scotian who was the daughter of another New York shipbuilder. Albenia, unlike Donald McKay, had the benefit of a fine education while growing up and she was particularly adept at mathematics, a subject that Donald McKay knew little about. Albenia had also gained a great deal of knowledge about shipbuilding from her father. Thus, Albenia was able to teach Donald about physics and mathematical knowledge, and the skills that he would require as a shipbuilder. In doing so she helped her husband to make his professional leap from being a craftsman to becoming a true naval architect. In nineteenth-century shipbuilding, the artisan or craftsman worked exclusively with solid materials to build a ship, usually by transposing the dimensions of a half-hull wooden model of a ship to the actual ship under construction in a shipyard. But a naval architect could also work with drawings by drafting the lines of a ship on paper with full knowledge of the necessary mathematics and of the descriptive words, marks, abbreviations, and conventions of nautical design. With her husband,

Albenia spent many evenings experimenting with the design of ships and analyzing ship construction techniques.

Meanwhile, in 1843, an American shipbuilder named John W Griffiths, who was employed at the Smith and Dimon Shipyard in New York, and who is said to have given lectures on shipbuilding, argued for a new type of ship — a rakish and narrow-hulled design that would emphasize speed. His lectures are credited with influencing the design of the first true clipper, the *Rainbow*, launched in 1845, which, along with her sister, the *Sea Witch*, showcased steeply raked bows and placed a ship's greatest width aft. *Rainbow* proved to be a good sailor and a fast ship and she would lead the way towards the subsequent development of the true, or extreme clippers. The McKays became friends with John Griffiths and they tossed shipbuilding ideas back and forth with him at dinners that brought together the McKays with other young shipbuilders in New York.

Donald McKay studied closely the design and building of the *Rainbow*. He took careful note of her unique characteristics, which included a concave bow at the waterline, a long, slender hull, and the positioning of her greatest width much farther towards the stern than previous designs. McKay now dreamed of building great ships along the new design to achieve the most speed — ships that would be the greyhounds of the seas.

But Donald McKay's career took a fateful turn when he left

the Brown and Bell Shipyard to take up a position at the US Navy Yard in New York. There, McKay, a Canadian, ran afoul of antipathy towards foreigners holding a sensitive position and when the shipyard staff refused to work with him he was forced out of his employment. Brown and Bell came to his rescue, however, by giving him a commission to construct two ships in Maine. His commission to build the two ships in Maine for Brown and Bell in Maine was successful, and in his sojourn in New England, the Nova Scotian felt more at home than in New York. He decided to stay in New England and he and Albenia settled in Newburyport, Massachusetts, to build ships and to raise a family.

After several short-lived business partnerships around Newburyport Donald McKay decided that he wanted to open his own shipyard, a dream that he was encouraged to pursue by a new customer, American shipping magnate Enoch Train. So the McKays moved to East Boston where McKay started his shipyard, forging a business relationship with Enoch Train who would give McKay's yard multiple orders, including some orders for extreme clippers for Train's transatlantic service.

In East Boston McKay designed and built his greatest achievements in shipbuilding, taking advantage of Boston's closeness to good lumber, and its eager reception of new technologies in shipbuilding. McKay's timing was perfect because historical forces at mid-century now combined to promote a great demand for speed. By mid-century Britain was moving decidedly away from its previous mercantilist economic approaches as large monopoly firms such as the East India Company and Hudson's Bay Company began to lose their monopolies. While monopolists did not require speedy shipping (because they were monopolists) traders in competitive markets did, and they placed a premium on speed. On land, railways began to be constructed in Britain and then elsewhere and they cut land travel times considerably. At sea, a Collins steamship was able to cross the Atlantic in less than 10 days in 1851. Slowly but surely, the world was becoming smaller.

When gold was discovered at Sutter's Mill in the new US military-governed territory of California in 1848, the great California gold rush was on. In the absence of an overland route to California from the eastern United States, all traffic to the gold fields of California had to go by sea around Cape Horn. Then, in 1851, gold was discovered in Australia, sparking a second gold rush on the shores of the Pacific Ocean. Later there would be additional gold rushes into the Cariboo country of British Columbia, and at Otago, in New Zealand. The gold rush traffic instantly created a market demand for new ships capable of a fast passage. The result would be the full evolution of the extreme clipper ship. In 1850 the transit time to California from New York was 159 days but just one year later it would fall far below that as shipbuilders began to build clipper ships. The *Sea Witch*, the masterful creation of John W. Griffiths, would soon make the passage from New

York to San Francisco in the then-unheard-of time of only 97 days.

At mid-century, the extreme clipper emerged from draughtsmen's tables to claim pride of place among sailing ships on the world's oceans. The clipper ship was the perfect example of form following function. But just what defined a clipper and made it different from other ships? A sailor's definition of a clipper ship had two components. Firstly, she needed to display sharp lines, tall masts, and the ability to carry a vast amount of sails. And secondly, she had to use those sails consistently to go as fast as possible across the world's oceans. A shipbuilder's definition would probably also have included the clipper's strengthened keelson, which was mounted on the ship's keel. A clipper's keelson included three riders atop the original, strengthening the ship. That was important because the ship's masts were fixed to the keelson, and the vast sail area of a clipper caused additional pressure to be placed on the hull through the keelson.

Speed was essential in the Pacific passenger trade and also for trade in products that were potentially subject to spoilage, such as tea from China. Factors such as speed, hull strength, cargo capacity, and economy (and for the passenger trade, luxury) had to be combined in a way that resulted in both optimal performance and a beautiful ship. The ships that Donald McKay now envisaged would be suitable for long voyages where strong winds would be common, and where quick passages were sought by shippers and passengers.

Speed can be defined by the total time that a ship spends in a passage between two ports, by the ship's speed per hour, or by the distance covered by a ship in a single day or week. Maximum speed was achieved when a sailing ship took the best possible advantage of high winds but average speed spread over the whole voyage was actually more important from an economic viewpoint. Some clipper ships did well in light winds but had to shorten sail in heavy winds while others were required to sail at great angles to the wind when they encountered headwinds. Such characteristics might therefore reduce the average speeds obtainable by such ships over the course of an entire voyage.

The maximum speed of a ship is a function of a ship's length on the waterline. The crest of a bow wave as a ship moves through the water increases in length the faster a ship moves through the sea and at a certain point the stern of the ship cannot be held high above the wave and the ship has to climb above her bow wave. A ship that has to climb above its bow wave requires a significant driving force to do that but a ship having a long hull length can achieve a higher speed, given perfect conditions, before she is forced to clamber over her bow wave. In approaching the design of his first clipper Donald McKay would have been aware of such factors but he would also have had to consider and make allowance for the strength of a ship and its stability in high winds.

Donald McKay was now ready to build the first of his version of this new type of ship —the extreme clipper — one that matched to the greatest degree the characteristics of a clipper ship as proposed by John Griffiths. McKay's racehorses of the seas would be subsequently viewed as the epitome of sailing ship design and his ships would obtain the greatest speeds that were achievable by full-rigged ships harnessing the power of the wind. But such ships would also be costly to operate and complex to handle, especially since they would carry 20 or more big sails and a mass of sail rigging that would require large crews to operate. Rigging technology changed during this period because the Crimean War 1853-56, cut off supplies of Russian hemp to Europe and accelerated the adoption of stronger wire rope in a ship's standing rigging, especially for the stays, shrouds and backstays that supported the masts Stays give fore and aft support to the masts, shrouds provided side to side support for the masts and the backstays gave diagonal support to the rear of the masts and provided most of the stability of the masts when the sails were deployed. Wire rope was superior to hemp because it could withstand the heavier wind pressures experienced by the clippers, thus encouraging the adoption of taller masts and a greater mass of sails.

McKay forged ahead with his plans but now he would do so now without the support of his wife Albenia, who died in childbirth before McKay obtained his greatest public recognition for ship design. McKay would subsequently remarry and his second wife, Mary Cressy Litchfield, had a poetic bent of mind and it was she who suggested many of the mellifluent names that were attached to McKay's clipper ships. Beginning with the *Stag Hound* in 1850, Donald McKay would craft a series of extreme clippers that were universally acclaimed for their speed, grace, and beauty on the high seas. A testament to Donald McKay's skill as a builder is shown by the fact that of thirteen clipper ships recording single-day runs that exceeded 400 miles twelve of those clippers were designed and built by Donald McKay.

The *Stag Hound* was 226 feet in length, three-masted with a 200-foot high mainmast, and was capable of spreading 11,000 square yards of sail. McKay built her in only 60 days at East Boston, giving her a rakish bow five feet higher than her stern and gracing her with a gilded stag hound as a figurehead. She proved to be a successful ship. McKay followed her up with his most famous ship, the *Flying Cloud*, a clipper that was renowned for her beauty but which also proved to be a very fast ship. Under Captain Josiah Perkins Creesy, who always went to sea with his navigator wife Eleanor Prentiss Creesy, *Flying Cloud* set out from New York on June 2, 1851, on a history-making voyage to San Francisco that saw the ship reach the Golden Gate 89 days and 21 hours after leaving New York, a record voyage. In 1854, still under the redoubtable Captain Creesy and his navigator wife, Eleanor, *Flying Cloud* would beat her own record and voyage from New York to San Francisco in 89 days and eight hours, a record that would stand for 140 years!

The "Flying Cloud"

Flying Cloud

McKay's *Lightning* once travelled 436 miles in a single day between Boston and Liverpool, an astonishing record. That was exceeded only by McKay's *Champion of the Seas*, which would be remembered for logging the best one-day run by a clipper ship in 1854 — 465 miles from 12 noon to 12 noon in the Indian Ocean on December 11, 1854. During that run, she reached a speed of 20 knots. For sheer speed, the *Champion of the Seas* would be exceeded only by McKay's clipper *James Baines*, which achieved a speed of 21 knots while sailing west of Cape Horn on the Melbourne to Liverpool run on June 18, 1856, although McKay's *Sovereign of the Seas* would also claim a speed of 22 knots on a London to Sydney voyage in 1854.

McKay's designs placed his ship's centres of buoyancy further towards their sterns and gave them slightly raked sternposts.

He also provided his creations with flatter bottoms. Those features, a centre of buoyancy farther aft, and flattened bottoms, contributed to the stability and strength of his ships, thus enabling them to carry a greater mass of sails. That, coupled with the sharp, rakish bows of his clippers, and their slightly rounded forefoot where the stem joined to the keel, meant that his ships would slice through the waves with greater power, especially in strong winds, and thus enable his ships to maximize their speed potential. McKay's designs made his ships very popular with those shipping companies in the United States and Great Britain that offered destinations to the west coast of North America, or to Australia, where strong winds were sure to be encountered in the seas that were frequented by the clipper ships.

Donald McKay remained a meticulous man who constantly sought to improve on his designs. He once said: "I never yet built a vessel that came up to my own ideal. I saw something in each ship which I desired to improve upon."[3]

Donald McKay

McKay proved to be the right man at the right time because the triumph of the extreme clipper ship would last little more than a decade, from 1850 until just after the outbreak of the American Civil War (although British clippers would last somewhat longer). Some 250 clipper ships of all types would be built in American yards and many of the best of them emerged from Donald McKay's shipyard in East Boston. His creations were hailed in his own time, and in ours, as the most beautiful combinations of wood and sail to ever grace the oceans.

Notes

1. *Quoted in Men, Ships and the Sea, 1973, p. 217.*
2. *Transatlantic Train, p. 46.*
3. *Donald McKay, quoted in Barons of the Sea, p. 231.*

The Wind And The Sails

2

Chapter 2. Samuel Cunard and the Rise of the Steamship

While Donald McKay was growing up in Nova Scotia and embarking on a successful career as a master shipbuilder in the United States another Canadian from Nova Scotia was following an entirely different vision for shipbuilding and world trade. He was a shy, self-effacing man from Halifax who foresaw at an early point in the nineteenth century that steam power would ultimately supplant sail power on the world's oceans, and he worked avidly for that day to come. His name was Samuel Cunard and he was born on November 21, 1787, in Halifax, to a family that was descended from German Quakers who had emigrated to Pennsylvania in 1683. A family of farmers, they struck it rich when their plough upturned a bag of gold coins that were thought to be from a pirate's treasure trove, giving rise to a myth about the family's good luck. But the family's luck changed when the Revolutionary War broke out and public sentiment in America turned against ideological pacifists such as the Quakers. Continental Army troops were billeted in Quaker homes against a homeowner's will and Quaker horses and blankets were requisitioned for the military struggle against the Crown. Financial penalties were also exacted from the Quakers for their failure to pledge allegiance to the rebel cause or to muster for enlistment in the Continental Army. As the war turned more favourably towards the rebel cause the future of the Cunard family appeared bleak and they fled to British-held New York City for refuge. When the subsequent British defeat at the Battle of Yorktown spelled the end of British colonial America, the family evacuated to Canada with other loyalists, settling in Nova Scotia. Although many of the Quaker loyalists settled around Shelburne, Nova Scotia, where Donald McKay would subsequently be born, Samuel's branch of the Cunard family settled in Halifax. Samuel's father, Abraham, may have felt partially isolated from his Quaker community because of his marriage to Margaret Murphy, the daughter of a loyalist soldier from South Carolina who was of Irish descent and a Roman Catholic. Abraham supported his family as a carpenter by building houses and working for the British Army garrison in Halifax.

Samuel Cunard grew up to be a self-disciplined but shy and reserved young man. He obtained a start in trade by buying and selling general merchandise until his father was able to obtain a position for him in the Royal Dockyard where he learned all about ships. Thereafter, a sojourn in Boston, Massachusetts, working for a shipbroker, taught him much about the shipping business. Cunard returned to Halifax where he went into business with his father as a ship agent specializing in the West Indies trade. Their firm profited from the War of 1812, as Halifax remained the most important British military bastion in eastern North America with a large army garrison and multiple Royal Navy fleet units. During the war, the Cunard firm purchased its first square-rigger at a prize auction, the *White Oak*, and placed her into transatlantic cargo service.

After the war, Samuel Cunard obtained a mail contract for the carriage by sea of the Royal Mail between Bermuda, Halifax, and St. John's, Newfoundland (subsequently extended to Boston). In the role of a carrier of the Royal Mail Samuel Cunard established a longstanding reputation for reliability that would continue to follow him into the great shipping firm that he later founded. His reputation for reliability doubtless helped him to also secure a contract as an official agent for the East India Company, which gave his business a significant source of revenue. Over time Cunard would engage in many trades connected to the shipping business including whaling, coal, lumber, warehousing, and banking, all of them generally to his profit. Cunard also invested heavily in real estate.

From his offices in Halifax Cunard became curious about an innovation in marine transport — the steam engine. The first steam engines appeared in England in the eighteenth century in the form of the Newcomen Engine. However, it was James Watt and his later invention of a separate condenser for steam engines that allowed a piston to provide the economical power that made the steam engine a practical device.

The use of steam to power vessels in North America first came to fruition in New York in 1807, when Robert Fulton's steamboat, the *Clermont*, embarked passengers for excursions along the Hudson River. A prominent Montreal businessman, John Molson, saw the *Clermont* on the Hudson River and he became intrigued by the concept. He arranged for the construction of a steam vessel on the St. Lawrence River in Lower Canada (Quebec) that was named *Accommodation*, and which, in 1809, became the first steamboat on the St. Lawrence River. Later Molson would build an even larger steamboat, the *Swiftsure*, with a length of 130 feet and a beam of 24 feet.

Although the conquest of the Great Lakes by steam propulsion was interrupted by the War of 1812, by 1816 there was a regular steamship service on Lake Ontario, followed by Lake Erie in 1818, and then Lake Huron in 1822. Steam was also first used on the ocean in 1818, when an American auxiliary steamship, the *Savannah*, voyaged from New York to Liverpool using steam for a total of 80 hours during her 27-day voyage.

In Halifax, Samuel Cunard took an interest in a small steam

ferry, the *Sir Charles Ogle*, operating between Halifax and Dartmouth, Nova Scotia, and he thought about the wider possibilities of steam transportation. He realized that auxiliary steam meant that there would be at least a partial relief from the vicissitudes of the weather at sea, and that augured well for the future of the shipping business. When the colonial governments of Lower Canada (Quebec) and Nova Scotia offered subsidies for a steam service Cunard cast about for a consortium to build and operate a steamship service between the colonies. The consortium he created was successful, and a contract was let to a Quebec shipbuilder to construct an interprovincial steamship. The result was the 1370-ton *Royal William*, with dimensions of 160 feet in length and 44 feet in breadth, which was rigged as a three-masted schooner but also equipped with twin paddle wheels. Her two-cylinder steam engine could produce 200 horsepower. She was launched in 1831 and fitted out at Montreal. In August 1831, she departed Quebec for Halifax, making the voyage in six and one-half days. In Halifax, Samuel Cunard frequently visited the *Royal William*. But ultimately this first foray into steam power proved uneconomic for Cunard, and the interprovincial steamship service went bankrupt. The *Royal William* was sold at a public auction.

When the *Royal William's* new owners were unable to find a way to make the ship pay, they decided to sail her to Britain and try to sell the ship there. On August 18, 1833, the *Royal William* departed Pictou, Nova Scotia, with seven passengers and 324 tons of coal. Burning coal all the way (except when her engines were down for maintenance) the *Royal William* made the first transatlantic crossing (mostly) by steam by an auxiliary steamship. The voyage of the *Royal William* established the efficacy of steam propulsion for lengthy sea voyages, a fact that certainly did not escape Samuel Cunard's attention.

Royal William

Meanwhile, Cunard's businesses, including his shipping interests, continued to prosper in the maritime provinces and Samuel Cunard was now a member of the provincial elite, having been appointed to the Legislative Council of Nova Scotia, the most important political institution in the province because it collectively served as the Governor's advisor on matters of public policy.

Samuel Cunard continued to watch the development of steam transportation technology and its potential application to the shipping industry, always searching for an opportunity where steam propulsion could enhance his shipping interests. In 1839, such an opportunity arose when the British Admiralty tendered for an improved mail service between Great Britain and North America using steamships capable of producing 300 horsepower. Formerly, the Admiralty had used slow sailing packets to carry the mail across the ocean to North America but sailing ships were unreliable, and the British ships were much slower than their American counterparts. As a result, the Americans were capturing much of the mail freight between the two continents.

The Admiralty's brief expression of interest in a steamship service stated:

"Steam vessels required for conveying Her Majesty's Mails and Despatches between England and Halifax (Nova Scotia), and also between England and Halifax and New York."[1]

Relying on his extensive previous experience carrying the colonial mail on the inter-coastal routes in North America Cunard proposed a twice-monthly mail service from England to Halifax by transatlantic steamships, with smaller steamships to carry the mail from Halifax to Boston where the United

States Postal Service could forward inbound mails to US destinations.

Fortuitously, the official at the Admiralty in charge of the project to create a steamship service to carry the Royal Mail across the Atlantic was an old acquaintance of Cunard. Captain Sir William Edward Parry was a famous explorer of Canada's arctic regions during the colonial period (the Parry Channel is named after him). Earlier in his career, between 1813-17, Parry had been assigned to the North American station based at Halifax where he and Samuel Cunard had become acquainted. Their relationship now gave credence to Cunard's approach to the Admiralty concerning the mail contract. After some negotiation, the Admiralty committed to support Cunard's proposed service with an annual subsidy of 55,000 pounds sterling (equivalent then to about $260,000.00 US dollars, and more than nine million US dollars today).

With his contract in hand, Cunard put together a consortium that included both Scottish shipbuilders on the Clyde River, and Scottish entrepreneurs. Four steamships of 1200 tons were built at the shipyards of John Wood and Robert Napier, and Robert Duncan. Those four steamships, *Acadia*, *Caledonia*, *Columbia*, and *Britannia* were able to generate approximately 440 horsepower from their steam engines, which was considerably above the 300 horsepower specified in the Admiralty's original specifications. Cunard planned to commence his scheduled transatlantic passenger and mail service in May 1840. The new company was to be known as The British and North America Royal Mail Steam Packet Company but from the outset it became known as Cunard's Line, and much later it would simply become the Cunard Line.

However, it was not until July 4, 1840, that Cunard's first transatlantic packet, the wooden three-masted paddle-wheeler *Britannia* actually sailed for North America with Samuel Cunard on board as a passenger. *Britannia* was a 207-foot bark-rigged auxiliary steamship built by Robert Duncan of oak and yellow pine on the Clyde River in Scotland. She offered a large deckhouse to passengers for dining and assembly and below deck there were separate cabins for her male and female passengers, with a shipboard capacity of 100 male passengers and 24 female passengers. *Britannia* could muster a speed of eight and one-half knots and she carried a crew of 90 for handling the sails, the steam engine, the Royal Mail, the passengers, and the freight.

On July 17, 1840, *Britannia* arrived at Halifax around two o'clock in the morning, following a 12-day voyage from Liverpool. After discharging her passengers and cargo *Britannia* continued on to America, arriving in Boston around 10:00 P.M. on July 18, 1840, to the accompaniment of fireworks. A public celebration was held on July 21st that was attended by two thousand Bostonians. A scheduled transatlantic steamship service was now in operation linking North America and Europe, proving the benefit of steam propulsion for reliability. Cunard's ships would make the transatlantic westbound crossing in an average of 11 days and eastbound crossings in an average of 13 days. At the public banquet celebrating Samuel Cunard's achievement the presiding dignitary, Josiah Quincy declared: "The enlightened foresight of Mr. Cunard, a citizen of Nova Scotia, aided by the liberality of the British Crown, has established a line of steam packets on a permanent basis."[2]

From that early start the Cunard company that Samuel Cunard formed with Scottish interests never really looked back, although Cunard did encounter some financial distress in the 1840s. But with the help of the Bank of Nova Scotia, he was able to overcome a financial crisis. He was nevertheless compelled to seek (and obtain) a renegotiation of the terms of his agreement with the Admiralty to take into account his unanticipated costs. By 1844, the Cunard line was becoming profitable. Over time, the Cunard ships, always reliable and never flashy, would achieve dominance over other steamship lines, and over the sailing ships in transatlantic service, thus pointing the way for the eventual triumph of steam over sail on the world's oceans.

Sir Samuel Cunard, Bart.

Notes

1. Quoted in *Transatlantic Train*, p. 38
2. Quoted in *Transatlantic*, p. XVI

THE WIND AND THE SAILS

3

Chapter 3. James Smith and the Marco Polo

As early as 1773, there was a burgeoning trade in lumber between the province of Nova Scotia (which at that time also included the territory that would later become New Brunswick) and Great Britain. That trade grew after the outbreak of the long wars with first Revolutionary, and then Napoleonic France, cut Britain off from her traditional Baltic suppliers of timber, thus forcing Britain to offer subsidies and customs relief on lumber imported from Canada.

More than any other factor the increase in the lumber trade between Canada and Great Britain fuelled the creation of a domestic shipbuilding industry in the maritime provinces, and a domestic shipping industry in the Canadian provinces. At the end of the War of the American Revolution in 1783,

300 vessels were registered in the maritime provinces of Canada, and by 1800, Nova Scotia shipyards alone had produced and registered more than 700 ships.

Canadian shipyards were also active along the St. Lawrence River in Lower Canada (Quebec) and around the Bay of Fundy, as well as on Prince Edward Island. Maritime Canadians, in particular, were drawn to the sea and shipbuilding by the happy coincidence of possessing vast forests, many harbours, and a well-positioned location close to the United States that was also complimented by lines of communication to Europe. Maritime residents were also versatile and many men could clear bush, farm, build a schooner, and sail it to New England with a cargo of produce. By building upon those capabilities shipbuilding became an important industry in maritime Canada. By 1878, more than one million tons of shipping were under registration in the maritime provinces, and at the century's end, almost 10,000 ships had been built in maritime Canada with the peak of production occurring in the 1850s. The city of St. John, New Brunswick, became the most important shipbuilding centre in maritime Canada although shipyards could also be found all around the Bay of Fundy, as well as in southern Nova Scotia, and on Prince Edward Island.[1]

Canadian shipbuilding yards specialized in building droghers, a rather large clumsy ship made from softwood lumber, primarily pine, tamarack (also called hackmatack), spruce, black birch, maple, and some white oak. The purpose of a drogher was to carry lumber, primarily boards and planks described as deal timber, to Great Britain. Droghers were built with bow and stern ports to facilitate the loading of the long and squared lumber into the ship's holds. Droghers were flat-sided ships that provided plenty of space for loading lumber cargoes and although slow and ugly they were designed to plough into waves and roll about them to force their way forward. Some droghers were so roughly made that they were intended to be broken up for their lumber after only a single voyage from North America to Britain. For that reason, European shipbuilders often deprecated Canadian ships that were so unlike the masterful oak and teak products of European shipbuilders.

But Canadians could also build fine ships that stood the test of time. One man, James Smith, a shipbuilder in St. John, New Brunswick, thought about the ships produced in the Maritimes and while he agreed that good profits could continue to be made from producing droghers he also considered that more money might be made from producing a well-made ship that could answer the growing desire among passengers and shippers for more speed in sea passages. The first tea cargoes to arrive in Great Britain from China always obtained a market premium and the California and Australian gold rushes also showed that passengers would pay a premium to reach the goldfields quickly. Smith therefore decided to build a ship with the characteristics of both speed and carrying capacity that might secure time-sensitive cargoes at a profit.

The Wind And The Sails

Such a ship, he knew, might also be converted to carry passengers speedily, and at a premium fare.

The type of ship that Smith envisaged would later be called a medium clipper, a ship that incorporated many of the features of the fast ships that were then beginning to be produced south of the border by master shipbuilders along the eastern coast of the United States such as Donald McKay, but medium clippers could provide more carrying capacity than the true greyhounds of the sea that McKay's creations represented. The ship that Smith envisaged was one with a sharp bow, wider amidships than the norm but narrower below the waterline, and with a squared-off stern. Wider ships were favoured by Canadian shipyards because they provided greater cargo capacity, although such designs could also compromise a ship's speed.

Smith decided to build his new ship at Marsh Creek, a nondescript waterway that flowed into Courtenay Bay, a part of the larger Bay of Fundy, which has tidal variations that are among the largest in the world. At Marsh Creek, for example, the tidal variations reached 25 feet. It was, nevertheless, a muddy and swampy location. One observer described Marsh Creek as: ". . . the most God-forsaken hole possibly discovered, considering the fine ships that had been built there."[2]

James Smith's roots were in Ireland but he was born on the island of Guernsey in the Channel Islands in 1802. He was raised by an uncle after the death of his mother, his father being absent from his life. At seventeen he emigrated to New Brunswick with a cousin and spent two years working as a lumberjack near Grand Falls, New Brunswick, but after the death of his cousin, he moved to St. John. In St. John Smith took a job at a local shipyard to learn the shipbuilding trade and at twenty-five he married Margaret McMorran, an immigrant from County Down in Ireland. With her, he had seven children and although none of them would survive him he would be survived by his grandchildren. From 1836 to 1842, Smith merely acted as a contractor, working on projects for local shipbuilders, but after 1842 he established his own shipyard, taking his son, also named James, as a partner. By 1850 the shipyard of James Smith and Son had produced some 18 ships, primarily droghers, but also other merchant craft. His reputation as a shipbuilder became well-established not only in Canada but in Great Britain as well. Now, James Smith turned to his greatest project, the building of a ship that he would long be remembered for.

The ship that Smith planned would be around 180 feet in length, a three-decked ship with a half poop deck and capable of carrying large cargoes or, possibly, many passengers. The frame of a ship always determined the shape of a vessel and for this new ship, Smith envisaged that her ribs would be acutely tapered. When attached to the keel her shape would create an impression of a yacht, what the historian Joseph Schull would later describe as "the belly of an alderman on the legs of a ballet dancer."[3] Not everyone was enthusiastic about the design of the *Marco Polo*, however. Smith's ship would also be described as "square as a brick fore and aft, with a bow like a savage bulldog."[4]

Built of seasoned timbers she would have three masts and be square-rigged. Although fore and aft sails were suitable for ships in the coastal trade, Smith's new ship would be an ocean carrier and the square sails of a square-rigger were necessary to supply the driving force necessary to propel the ship at great speed on long ocean voyages. But she would also have a gaff, a fore and aft sail on her mizzen mast, to aid in ship control.

Smith began constructing his new ship in the autumn of 1850, and under his watchful eye, and the watchful eye of his foreman, John Fredrickson, fifty shipwrights worked from a half-ship model of the hull to build the actual ship doing everything by hand except for the cutting of boards, which was done by a steam-powered sawmill. Then, disaster struck. A gale swept into Courtenay Bay and wrecked the ship as it was standing on the shipyard stocks. The half-built ship collapsed but doggedly Smith and Fredrickson began to put her back together again and, hopefully, to make her stronger. Possibly, some of the frames of the ship, may not have been reinstalled in their proper order after the ship was wrecked on the stocks and it has been suggested that this may have in some way contributed to the great speed that the Marco Polo would subsequently display.[5]

Eighteen months later the ship was finished, with the specialized fittings such as steering, anchors, capstans, and with her binnacle installed last. She was 184.1 feet long (56.11 m.) with a beam of 36.3 feet (11.05 m.) and a depth of hold of 29.4 feet (8.96 m.). She was a three-decked ship with eight feet of headroom between her three decks. As a three-masted square-rigger she could deploy a spread of sails equal to 22,000 square feet (2000 square metres) and at her bowsprit, she boasted a life-size carving of her namesake, Marco Polo. Bow and stern ports were built into her hull to ease the loading of lumber into the ship. The finished ship towered over the shipyard as she stood in the stocks, and many marvelled at what was indeed the longest ship that had ever been built at St. John to that point in time. Awaiting the date of her proposed launch, the ship sat in a type of cradle with long wooden runners that surmounted the wooden slipway. Chains and ropes held her firmly in place until the launch date.

It was now April 1851 and it was decided to launch her on a spring tide which meant a slight delay in the timing of her launch but in the meantime, her lower masts, and the stays, backstays, and shrouds of her rigging could be installed to save time later during her fitting out.

Notes

1. *For a detailed descripiton of Canadian shipbuilding practices in the nineteenth century see Garth Wilson, A History of Shipbuilding and Naval Architecture in Canada, pp. 15-23.*

2. *Quoted in Wooden Ships and Iron Men, p. 45.*
3. *Quoted in Heritage of Canada, p. 259.*
4. *Quoted in Colonial Clippers, p. 27.*
5. *See Hollenberg, Marco Polo at p. 21 on this point.*

4

Chapter 4. A Botched Launching and a Maiden Voyage

There were more than a few who marvelled at the *Marco Polo* taking shape on the stocks of James Smith's shipyard. Some called her 'James Smith's Folly,' and decried her as something of an ugly duckling of a ship. Many thought that her design was a mistake and that she would never pay for her owners. But Smith remained adamant as he waited with the crowd of onlookers on April 17, 1851, as the final preparations for her launch into Marsh Creek were undertaken. The tall black ship conveyed strength, but not necessarily beauty, as she prepared to take to the water. A woman (perhaps Smith's wife) smashed a bottle of champagne across the bow of the ship and formally christened her as the *Marco Polo*. Then, shipwrights with axes chopped away at her restraining blocks. And then — nothing, as the ship did not move. A ram of logs was employed to try to force her down the shipyard ways and into the water but it was not until Smith's foreman, John Fredrickson, dislodged a small cleat that the *Marco Polo*, after much delay, finally began to move stern first into the water of an already receding tide.

Whether it was the weight of the ship as she slid down the ways or the force that was employed to start her moving the *Marco Polo* entered the water at a significant speed. She rushed across Marsh Creek and embedded herself in the mud of the far bank and then careened over onto her side. While lying on her side the ship's frame was now no longer in alignment. Her keel twisted and distended, and curved inward, leaving her keel at amidships permanently six inches (15 cm) higher than the position of the keel at her bow and stern — a condition called hogging.

With the twisting and hogging she received at her unfortunate launching many now said that *Marco Polo* was a ruined ship, although there were some, perhaps more guarded in their assessments, who may have suggested that such a ship sometimes sailed faster as a result of a twist in her spine. Principles of ship design, however, did not support the proposition that a hogged ship should sail faster as a result. Nevertheless, in subsequent years suggestions were sometimes made that the *Marco Polo's* distended hull was the real reason for her fast sailing speeds. And so a legend grew up that the Marco Polo's misshapen keel was the key to understanding her famous speed. While there is no objective evidence to suggest that hogging explained the ship's performance the legend that the ship's misshapen spine somehow contributed to her speed has become part of the mystery and romance surrounding the story of the *Marco Polo*.

For James Smith the mis-launch of the *Marco Polo* was a veritable disaster. He nevertheless moved swiftly to recover his ship. For a fortnight he and his crews laboured to release the ship from the banks of Marsh Creek. Tons of mud had to be removed and trenches had to be dug along the sides of the ship to right her. Finally, a local tug, the *Sea Lion*, was employed to pull her off while crews continued digging her out at the stern of the ship. With all those exertions the ship was finally released from her imprisonment and the *Marco Polo* floated free. Once afloat, the ship was secured to a rigging wharf and the necessary work to complete the installation of her spars, rigging, and sails took place. Unlike many of the square-rigged ships of that era, the *Marco Polo* boasted one special technological advancement. She was fitted with a roller reefing topsail system patented by an inventor named Henry Cunningham which allowed the topsails to be reefed (that is, shortened) from the deck of the ship rather than by sending men aloft to shorten the sails in heavy weather. The Cunningham system lowered the yard and rotated it at the same time which resulted in the sail being wrapped around the yard. The result was a considerable increase in time savings and in crew safety.

The Wind And The Sails

On May 26, 1851, James Smith proudly registered his creation in the New Brunswick Ship Registry as:

"Ship Marco Polo, 1625 61/100 tons. Three decks and a half-poop. Length: 184.1 ft. Breadth amidships: 36.3 ft. Depth of hold amidships: 29.4 ft. Standing bowsprit. Square-sterned. No galleries. Owned by James Smith and James Thomas Smith."[1]

Now that she was ready to commence her role as a lumber carrier *Marco Polo's* bow and stern ports were opened and she was loaded with lumber for export, as well as some scrap iron. The ship settled well in the water and some of those who once thought that the ship appeared ungainly now reconsidered their views, seeing that in the water and fully loaded she at least no longer appeared to be an ugly duckling even if she was not quite a swan.

Ship "MARCO POLO," 1625 tons.
Built 1851, St. John, N.B.
(From an old painting.)

The *Marco Polo* under sail

On May 31, 1851, under the command of Captain William Thomas, aged 27, of St. John, the *Marco Polo* departed from St. John with all sails set, displaying a cloud of white canvas against a blue sky. *Marco Polo* made the crossing to Liverpool in fifteen days, which was a very respectable crossing time in that era. James Smith was interested in selling the *Marco Polo* but he found that the British shipowners were unenthused. The *Marco Polo* was still considered to be an unattractive ship and she was built of Canadian softwood, which was another mark against her in comparison to the British-built ships that were traditionally built of oak and teak. Furthermore, the knowledge of the *Marco Polo's* botched launching, and the resulting hogging of her spine, had preceded the *Marco Polo* to England, making British shipowners extra cautious in considering the merits of the ship. Despite that, Marco Polo received a favourable review in the *Illustrated London News*, which said of her:

"The distinguishing feature of the Marco Polo is the peculiarity of her hull. Her lines fore and aft are beautifully fine, her bearings are brought well down to the bilge; thus, whilst she makes amidships a displacement that will prevent unnecessary 'careening,' she has an entrance as sharp as a steamboat and a run as clean as can be conceived. Below the draught line her bows are hollow; but above she swells out handsomely, which gives ample space on the topgallant fo'c's'le — in fact, with a bottom like a yacht, she has above water all the appearance of a frigate."[2]

James Smith sent the ship in ballast from Liverpool to Mobile, Alabama, to procure a cargo of cotton, which was safely brought to port in Liverpool by Captain Amos Cosby, a native of Yarmouth, Nova Scotia, who replaced Captain Thomas in Mobile. By all reports, the *Marco Polo* was a good sailing ship. Still, British shipowners remained uninterested and James Smith transferred his share in the ship to his son and departed New Brunswick for Liverpool, where he was determined to make a sale of the ship. In the meantime, the *Marco Polo* languished in the Mersey River with a broom at her mast to advertise the fact that she was for sale.

THE WIND AND THE SAILS

[1] Quoted in – In the Wake of the Windships, at p. 45

[2] Quoted in The Colonial Clippers, p. 26

Chapter 5. Enter James Baines

As the *Marco Polo* lay in the Mersey River, one man spied an opportunity. Paddy McGee was a sometime rag merchant, ship chandler, and fertiliser merchant who also had a managerial role in connection with a few ships serving in the Australian trade. Taking advantage of *Marco Polo*'s somewhat dubious reputation, and the consequent lack of interest in her by the major Liverpool shipowners, McGee offered James Smith a modest price for the ship. With no other offers arising, Smith felt compelled to accept McGee's price. McGee was a general businessman rather than a true shipowner however and having obtained the ship at a bargain price he planned to flip the ship to someone else who was immersed in the shipping trade. McGee had a particular person in mind.

McGee approached James Baines, an up-and-coming Liverpool shipowner who owned the Black Ball Line. McGee thought that Baines might be interested in the vessel as a passenger carrier, given the great size of the *Marco Polo*. James Baines was born in Liverpool in 1823, to a family involved in the confectionery business. He was raised by his mother after the death of his father and he began to work for an uncle who was a shipbroker after his coming of age. Under his uncle's tutelage, Baines learned all he needed to know about the shipping business. Baines was both smart and easy to meet and he proved to be an excellent deal-maker, although he could also display a streak of ruthlessness when circumstances required it. He married in 1848, at the age of twenty-five to a local woman, Anne Browne, with whom he would have a son and three girls. The following year, in 1849, he started his own shipping company under the name of James Baines & Co., and by 1851 Baines had also joined forces with a local shipbuilder, Thomas Miller MacKay, and one William C Miller, to start the Black Ball Line (a name Baines apparently purloined from an American firm). Baines also enjoyed a good working relationship with the captain of one of his ships, Robert Nicol Forbes, otherwise known to sailors as 'Bully' Forbes.

Baines had earlier purchased some ships that had been built in the Canadian Maritimes, and Quebec, and he was therefore quite familiar with the capabilities of Canadian shipbuilders. With the discovery of gold in Australia a great gold rush down under was underway and seeing the need for speedy ships to carry passengers to Australia, Baines was immediately interested in the *Marco Polo*.

McGee invited Baines to come and inspect his new vessel and Baines agreed to view the ship. McGee put forward his best salesman's pitch to Baines. Now envisaging the possibilities of turning the *Marco Polo* from a freighter into a passenger ship for the Australian trade, Baines returned the following day bringing along his trusted captain James Nicol Forbes. Captain Forbes, who had sailed as a master of Canadian-made droghers, went all over the ship, spending a total of five hours conducting a thorough inspection. Forbes was impressed with the ship and probably realised that her shapeliness underwater would propel her through the sea at a significant speed. On Forbes's recommendation, James Baines bought the *Marco Polo* from Paddy McGee.

Baines dry-docked the *Marco Polo* and began the complex and expensive process of converting the ship from a lumber drogher into a passenger ship. Baines knew that potential passengers would pay for speed but that they also wanted comfort on a long voyage so he decided to make the *Marco Polo* as luxurious and attractive a carrier as possible. It seems that at this time her exterior decorations were supplemented with carvings at her stern evoking the inveterate Venetian explorer for whom the ship was named, one showing Marco Polo in repose, as well as carvings of a star and an elephant recalling his travels. The ship's bottom was copper-sheathed, and partitions were built throughout the interior to create the private cabins, wide staircases, and salons that passengers would expect. The interior design of the ship featured red carpeting and red velvet upholstery throughout the passenger areas. With the addition of paintings, artistic glasswork and gilt and silver accents the reconditioned *Marco Polo* projected luxury. The *Illustrated London News* examined the vessel in its reconditioned form and reported:

"Her timbering is enormous. Her deck beams are huge balks of pitch-pine. Her timbers are well formed and ponderous. The stem and stern frame are of the choicest material . . . On deck forward of the poop, which is used as a ladies' cabin, is a home on deck to be used as a dining cabin. It is ceiled with maple, and the pilasters are panelled with richly ornamented and silvered glass, coins of various countries being a feature of the decorations . . . a sheet of plate glass with a cleverly painted picturesque view in the centre, with a framework of foliage and scroll in the opaque colours and gold . . . the saloon doors are panelled in stained glass bearing figures of commerce and industry . . ." [1]

James Baines had taken a great financial risk in converting the *Marco Polo* from a lumber drogher into a passenger ship and he was now heavily indebted. In doing so Baines had relied on large loans from Barneds Bank. But Baines thought he could recoup the money he put into the Marco Polo from the burgeoning demand for passage to Australia, which was now fuelled by gold fever.

As the *Marco Polo* waited in the Mersey to begin her life as a passenger ship on the Great Britain to Australia run James Baines convened a Liverpool tradition, a great pre-voyage banquet, at which rival shipowners and captains good-naturedly roasted James Baines and his new master of the *Marco Polo*, Captain James Nicol Forbes. Among those in attendance was at least one banqueter who would have hoped for Baines's success with the *Marco Polo*. As the ship's builder, James Smith was there in person to witness the transformation of the *Marco Polo* into a marvellous passenger vessel. Samuel Cunard's firm was also represented at the banquet and the Cunard representative spoke about the impressive size of the *Marco Polo* and noted that she was the largest ship that had ever been sent from Britain to Australia. He expressed the hope that she would also prove to be the most prosperous. While Baines remained coy as to how he thought his new ship would perform, Captain Forbes was boastful about the *Marco Polo*. Sure of himself, and of his new ship, Forbes laid a wager with the captain of the steam packet *Australia* that the *Marco Polo* would beat the *Australia* to Melbourne. Then Forbes went much further by declaring openly that he would sail the *Marco Polo* to Melbourne and back within six months. Forbes caused an uproar with that declaration because no ship had been able to achieve such a fast passage. Most ships took eight or nine months to sail to Melbourne and back and some took an entire year to make the voyage! Forbes accepted every wager that was offered by the assembled shipowners and ship captains, all of whom bet against his return within six months

The day after the pre-voyage banquet a tug came alongside the *Marco Polo* and took the ship down the Mersey River with a crew of 60 including the captain, four mates and two physicians. Some 930 passengers (750 of them government-sponsored emigrants) and their settlers effects were brought out to the ship lying in the Mersey by a small steam tender to begin *Marco Polo's* epic voyage. There was also a menagerie of live farm animals on board to provide food for the passengers in those pre-refrigeration days.

The passengers were carefully segregated according to sex, their civil status, and the transportation class that they had purchased. The forward cabins were set aside for single men, while the amidship cabins were set aside for families. Those cabins towards the stern of the ship were reserved for single women passengers. Within each of those groupings, those travelling in steerage class would be placed more forward within the group while those travelling in intermediate class would be placed more amidships. The highest class would be found in cabins located towards the stern and placed along the sides of the ship. Those 'cabin class' passengers also had access to the poop deck. As was traditional in sailing vessels, the crew quarters were in the bow of the ship and the officers' cabins were found in the stern of the ship.

Outward bound, *Marco Polo's* route would take her south

through the North Atlantic and on into the South Atlantic before passing the Cape of Good Hope and then traversing the Indian Ocean, en route to Australia.

[1] Quoted in Witch in the Wind at p. 43; Wooden Ships and Iron Men, p. 4; see also The Colonial Clippers p. 26.

Chapter 6. The Fastest Ship in the World

The fame of the *Marco Polo* as a ship is closely entwined with one man — James Nicol Forbes, her master during her history-making voyages to the southern continent. Forbes was a Scotsman who was born in Aberdeen in 1821. He was a five-foot-seven redhead who went to sea as a boy of twelve but it was not until he came to Liverpool in 1839, and began working on ships in the Canadian timber trade that his career accelerated. He developed a reputation as a colourful, if hot-tempered individual, boastful, and sometimes abusive towards others earning himself the sobriquet 'Bully' Forbes. But he was a fine sailor.

Over time Forbes worked his way up to the rank of master where he began to be taken note of by shipowners. His reputation as a ship captain was earned by making consistently good passages between Great Britain and Canada. A fine navigator, and a tough man, who was also a well-trained mariner who knew ships, knew sailors, and knew what he had to do to get the best results from both of them. In 1851, Forbes came to the notice of James Baines who hired him into his Black Ball Line as master of the *Cleopatra* and soon afterwards Baines came to rely on Forbes's knowledge and acumen about ships and the sea. Now, in 1852, Baines gave Forbes the command of the *Marco Polo*, his newest acquisition, and the most important ship in Baines's Black Ball Line.

James Forbes' boast at *Marco Polo's* farewell banquet that he would sail his ship to Australia and back in the then-unheard-of time of six months was not an idle boast. Forbes had held navigation discussions with officials of the Liverpool Marine Board and those officials had advised him that faster passages to the antipodean colonies might be obtained by following a great circle route instead of the more traditional Admiralty-prescribed routing.

For seventy years ships plying between Great Britain and Australia had followed a fixed compass route established by the Admiralty — a route that took at least 110 days. The Admiralty route went south from Britain to Tenerife in the Canary Islands and then on towards the Cape Verde Islands. From there it was a long southerly reach to Cape Town and the Cape of Good Hope, and then the Admiralty route turned east following the 39th parallel of latitude to Australia. It was a route that seemed on paper to be the most straightforward and practical but it was based on Mercator charts, and Mercator charts did not take into account the curvature of the Earth. The shortest route was one that could only be represented on a Mercator chart as a curved route.

One of the officials of the Liverpool Marine Board, a man named Towson, was a particular promoter of the use of the great circle routes and he had written a book on the subject. Forbes knew Towson and doubtless discussed with him the possibility of following a great circle route to Australia as an alternative to the prescribed Admiralty route.

Captain Forbes was also aware of the oceanographic and meteorological work that had been published by an officer of the United States Navy, Matthew Fontain Maury. After training at the US Naval Academy around 1825, Maury had secured an appointment in 1830 as a sailing master on the *USS Falmouth*, which had orders to proceed into the Pacific Ocean. As the ship's sailing master, Maury realized that it would be very desirable for him to consult any published records concerning the winds and currents of the Pacific Ocean. However, he soon discovered that there were no such public records, and faced with a paucity of published knowledge about the Pacific Ocean Maury resolved to make his own records, and to encourage other mariners to contribute their own knowledge to him as well.

Maury proceeded to create a form that he arranged to be

printed and distributed to the masters of other vessels going to the Pacific Ocean in hopes of acquiring as much information as possible. He also mined the marine records in the US naval archives in Washington. With all the information that Maury assembled he began to put together detailed charts of sea currents and air patterns for mariners, which proved to be remarkably accurate. In time, Maury became an acknowledged expert on currents and winds, and his charts were widely consulted by mariners. Maury famously became known as the 'Pathfinder of the Air.' By 1850, masters of vessels, including Forbes, were following established pathways in the oceans that took full advantage of the prevailing winds and currents based in large part on a lifetime of work by Matthew Fontain Maury.

On July 4, 1852, Captain Forbes took the *Marco Polo* to sea. A determined sailor, Forbes was constantly on deck examining the settings of *Marco Polo's* sails, and making such adjustments and trimmings of the ship's sails as would best capture the maximum amount of wind. Past the bulge of West Africa, the *Marco Polo* caught the southeast trade winds which carried her onwards until she passed 35 degrees South. There, she lounged about for a few days in the southern Indian Ocean waiting to catch the Westerlies some 700 miles south of the Cape of Good Hope that sped her east on her way to Australia. Forbes omitted the traditional stop at Cape Town that was usually made by ships following the Admiralty routing.

Forbes pressed on with a maximum spread of sail, including *Marco Polo's* mains, topsails, topgallants, royals, and skysails. Forbes also extended her yards by deploying the ship's studding sail booms and then he raised her studding sails. Showing his mettle and character as a courageous mariner Forbes was known to have had a habit aboard his ships of standing on a studding sail boom some 50 feet out from the hull of his ship and about 60 feet above the tossing waves of the ocean beneath him. It was an act of daring that could have easily sent him to the great beyond if the ship's helm had been only slightly mishandled by the helmsman.

With her sails under great pressure from the wind, it was probably no great surprise that some of the *Marco Polo's* yards snapped under the pressure, or that overly-taut sails burst, but Forbes quickly ordered repairs and kept pressing on. He was taking a route far to the south of the recommended Admiralty route in following a great circle route to the southern continent. By following a great circle route, and applying what he had gleaned from the investigations of the American navigator Matthew Maury, Forbes shaved 20% off of the traditional travel time between Great Britain and Australia. But his southern route brought his ship into the Roaring Forties, increasing the danger of an encounter with ice and also increasing the discomfort experienced by *Marco Polo's* passengers from the colder weather.

As Forbes drove the *Marco Polo* forward through the southern Indian Ocean, his ship achieved multiple daily runs exceeding

300 miles. When *Marco Polo* encountered a gale Forbes drove his ship through it for 96 hours without once reducing sail, displaying a tremendous confidence in the ship that James Smith had built. Finally, on September 18, 1852, some 76 days outward bound from her Liverpool anchorage the *Marco Polo* sighted Port Philips head, and two hours later she dropped anchor at Melbourne, Australia. The steam packet *Australia*, whose captain Forbes had bet that *Marco Polo* would beat to Melbourne arrived one week later.[1]

Upon entering Melbourne Harbour Forbes now displayed a streak of ruthlessness. The Australian gold rush was on and there were many ships in port languishing without crews because so many men had caught gold fever and had absconded to the gold fields to seek their fortunes. Forbes had no wish to be caught out without a crew to man his ship like some of the other captains. Therefore, he concocted a ruse to ensure that his crew would not abscond to the gold fields en masse. He hoisted the police flag as *Marco Polo* glided to a halt in the harbour and he mustered his crew. When the local police quickly responded and boarded the *Marco Polo*, Forbes accused his crew of insubordination and demanded that the police incarcerate them. The charge of insubordination was entirely trumped up by Forbes and his crew was innocent but despite their protestations, the police believed the captain of the vessel and relocated the *Marco Polo's* crew to Her Majesty's Jail, where they languished for three weeks while Forbes worked to prepare the *Marco Polo* for her return journey to Great Britain.

Although his crew was furious with him (and with the police) their 21-day sojourn in the local jail allowed tempers to cool somewhat and they were all back on board the *Marco Polo* on October 11, 1852, and in reasonably good humour, all things considered, as the *Marco Polo* prepared to depart Melbourne after a 24-day sojourn in Australia.

Forbes wasted no time in putting the *Marco Polo* back out to sea and by the next day, October 12, the *Marco Polo* was in Banks Strait outward bound from Australia and heading for Cape Horn. The *Marco Polo* passed by the Auckland Islands on October 17 and then caught the Roaring Forties and subsequently dropped down to catch the Furious Fifties where there was a real danger of ice and icebergs.

The seas and the weather became dangerously rough but Forbes insisted on pushing his ship to her limits. He put locks on the sheets so that no one could surreptitiously loosen them and thereby reduce the ship's speed. During one famous period on the return trip Forbes was said to have manned the poop deck with a pistol in each hand driving himself, his crew, and his ship towards Cape Horn. *Marco Polo* once again made multiple daily runs exceeding 300 miles. Then, in the grip of a great gale, the ship made a run of 353 miles on the day that the *Marco Polo* passed by Cape Horn. Once well past Cape Horn the *Marco Polo* turned north and entered gentler and warmer seas on the final leg of her journey back to Great Britain.

After passing Cape Horn and Tierra Del Fuego at the southernmost part of South America the Marco Polo sighted a barque, seemingly abandoned, and an empty lifeboat. Unable to raise the ship despite showing blue lights and firing rockets Forbes pressed forward through the Atlantic Ocean to Great Britain, leaving that mystery behind.

Marco Polo reached Holyhead, Wales, on the afternoon of Christmas Day, 1852, and then reached the Mersey River, and Liverpool, on the following day, which was Boxing Day, 1852. She had made the passage from Melbourne to Liverpool in 76 days, and her total time for a round-trip transit between Britain and Australia was 175 days, which translated into five months and 21 days — an incredible and unheard-of achievement in the middle years of the nineteenth century.

On Boxing Day, James Baines was stopped in the street by a report that the *Marco Polo* had been seen off Holyhead on Christmas Day. Baines was skeptical, and he initially scoffed at such a report. But, intrigued perhaps, he went down to the Salthouse Dock and was standing there on the banks of the Mersey River when a tug brought in his ship. Between the masts of the *Marco Polo*, Captain Forbes had hung a great sailcloth banner. Upon it was written the words "Fastest Ship in the World."

Marco Polo had made the entire journey well under the six

months that Forbes had boasted that he could do at the farewell banquet before *Marco Polo* departed from England. Once again, she had beaten the steamer *Australia* back from the southern continent.

Marco Polo's historic voyage had resulted in a round trip of only 175 days, including her 24-day layover in Melbourne. She had reached average speeds of more than 300 miles per day during many 24-hour periods and her best day saw her cover 364 miles, with her officers claiming that Marco Polo could reach 17 knots.

A sea passage from Britain to Australia in less than six months was sensational and both the *Marco Polo* and Forbes were instantly famous throughout Great Britain, and, subsequently, across the Atlantic in Canada and the United States. Previously, it had taken ordinary ships more than 110 days from Liverpool to reach Australia (and 123 days if they departed from London). Crowds now flocked to see the *Marco Polo* in the Mersey River and Captain Forbes was presented with a silver tea service and a silver candelabrum in recognition of his historic achievement. A fast passage to the far side of the world seemed to many to have made the world a smaller place. Many media articles were published about the *Marco Polo*, and a sizeable cottage industry of souvenirs and collectibles emerged to capitalize on her reputation. Throughout the country, and in the larger Atlantic community, the *Marco Polo* was celebrated. Her success also made a name in Great Britain for Canadian-built ships. New orders for ships from maritime Canada shipyards would soon follow, boosted by the gold rush fever and, later, by the outbreak of the Crimean War that once again cut off Baltic timber supplies to Britain.

Still, there could be skeptics and to allay any suspicions that he had merely been lucky Forbes prepared the *Marco Polo* for another fast voyage to Australia. Over the winter months, the *Marco Polo* was refitted and prepared for her second voyage to the antipodes, and by early March the ship was ready. It was considered that too many passengers were taken aboard for *Marco Polo's* initial voyage to Australia and so for her second outbound voyage her passenger complement was capped at 648 passengers.

As he prepared to take the *Marco Polo* to sea one more time the boastful Captain Forbes assembled the ship's passengers before him and blasphemously declared: "On my last passage, I astonished the world. On this one, I intend to astonish God Almighty."[2]

On March 13, 1853, *Marco Polo* was put to sea again under Forbes' command. Once again following a great circle route and taking advantage of the maritime knowledge that Maury and others had bequeathed to the world, the *Marco Polo* made her second passage to Australia in 75 days. But her return voyage to Britain which began on June 10, 1853, was fraught with danger and delay. She was caught in ice south of Cape Horn and the ice ripped off her copper sheathing. Still, Forbes managed to drive the ship back to Liverpool on September 13, 1853, six months to the day from her outward-bound departure from Liverpool. It was a spectacular achievement even if it was a few days longer than her first voyage and not one to match his boastful blasphemes about astonishing God. All skepticism about the achievement of Forbes and the *Marco Polo* was now put to rest. Some in England even alleged that Forbes had found a new sea route to the southern continent, while others remembered the twist in *Marco Polo's* keel when she was launched and they wondered, implausibly, if that was in some way responsible for her fast speed.[3]

'Bully' Forbes had now proved his worth as a sea captain if ever there had been any doubt and James Baines rewarded him with the command of his newest ship, the extreme clipper *Lightning* that Donald McKay had built for Baines in Boston. Forbes would be a worthy master of *Lightning* and of several other ships that he would go on to command. He would make many noteworthy passages but he would never again reach the height of acclaim that he received with his two extraordinarily fast passages to Australia in command of the *Marco Polo*.

[1] Some sources use the alternative criteria of the date Liverpool dropped below Marco Polo's horizon to the date that Marco Polo sighted Melbourne to compute the number of days

for the outward-bound voyage. That alternative criterion gives a total time for the passage from Britain to Australia of 68 days. I have preferred to use the anchorage to anchorage criteria, resulting in a length of passage of 76 days.

[2] Quoted in The Saltwater Men, at p. 50

[3] Although there has always been some speculation that Marco Polo's hogging contributed to her speed the physics of ship design and performance do not lend credence to that proposition.

Chapter 7. Fifteen Thousand Australians

James Baines was convinced by the success of the *Marco Polo* that clipper ships were essential to meet the market demand for fast passages to the southern continent. He stretched his resources and ordered four extreme clippers from Donald McKay in Boston. McKay built for him the *Lightning*, which Baines gave to James Nicol Forbes as his new command, the *Champion of the Seas*, the *James Baines*, and the *Donald McKay*. All proved to be fine ships and were among the very best works done by Donald McKay. All four were three-masted, flattened-bottomed ships of about 2000 tons and the Black Ball Line was well-served by them.

After the departure of Forbes from the *Marco Polo* the ship's First Mate, Charles McDonnell, took command of the *Marco*

Polo and under his leadership, the *Marco Polo* made an outward-bound voyage to Australia from Liverpool in only 72 days — four days better than the best Liverpool-Melbourne voyage made by the *Marco Polo* when Forbes had command of her. That proved that the *Marco Polo* was indeed a special ship.

Still, captains were an important part of the speed equation and where ships were known for speed their captains were often accused of recklessness. The effects of different masters' skill and acumen had a bearing on the quest for speed and while some could demand and get fast passages from their ships others, perhaps less skilled, were less successful.

Four other masters of the Black Ball Line served on the *Marco Polo* following Captain McDonnell; Captain RW (Edward) Wild, Captain James Clarke (a native of St. John, New Brunswick, like the *Marco Polo* herself), Captain DH Johnstone, and Captain William M Arnold. All of them were, like Forbes, men who were capable of hard behaviour when confronted by unruly crewmen or drunken passengers. Well-disciplined crews encouraged critics to suggest that their captains were brutal but the crews themselves were hard men — often with criminal records, instincts, or predispositions, and tough handling of them was essential to maintain shipboard discipline.

Clipper captains drove themselves equally hard. Often they seemed to live for their ships — sometimes lashing themselves to a deck chair in heavy weather to continuously monitor the speed of their ships, and the pressure of the wind on her masts and hulls. To those men, the clipper ships seemed almost alive, with the groans and creaks in the hull and the whistling of the wind in the rigging communicating to them whether they were pushing their ships beyond the point where disaster lay.

Although the *Marco Polo* would always be known for making fast passages, she did not long retain her reputation as the fastest ship in the world after Captain Forbes surrendered his command. Those honours would pass to the American clippers produced by Donald McKay at his shipyard in East Boston. Still, over the years that followed the *Marco Polo* remained a steady and fast performer for the Black Ball Line between Great Britain and Australia, setting a standard on the route for speed and passenger comfort. Always lauded as a fast ship *Marco Polo* normally averaged 80-90 days on the outward and return legs of a round-trip journey to Australia from Great Britain. She could reach a speed of 16 knots on her best days (17 knots if her officer's claims were correct). Although the *Marco Polo* could not equal the fastest speeds of Donald McKay's extreme clippers, it was certainly true that the *Marco Polo* was very fast indeed for a medium clipper.

Marco Polo remained popular with emigrant passengers to the southern continent throughout the 1850s and 1860s. In part that was because the *Marco Polo* was a safe ship as well as a luxurious one. The Emigration Commissioners had mandated that passenger vessels between Great Britain and Australia should carry medical practitioners as part of their crews and despite the prevalent gaps in medical knowledge in the nineteenth century, the mortality rate on voyages to Australia was relatively low as a result (although an outbreak of measles on the *Marco Polo's* first voyage to Australia resulted in the deaths of 52 children, which led to a subsequent restriction against the carriage of small children on emigrant vessels). In part, the overall low mortality was due to an insistence by the medical practitioners on cleanliness and good ventilation in the ship — a requirement that doubtless saved lives on such a long voyage.

Between 1852 and 1867, *Marco Polo* carried approximately 15,000 passengers to Australia from Great Britain. Perhaps today one million Australians can trace their family's arrival in Australia to an ancestor who obtained their passage on the *Marco Polo*. But *Marco Polo's* passages were not always uneventful. A parted tow rope damaged her side on one occasion, and on another occasion, she suffered a collision with the barque *Glasgow* in the Mersey River in December, 1855.

The *Marco Polo* at Port in Australia

Passages south of Cape Horn could be particularly problematic due to ice. On one voyage *Marco Polo* passed by an iceberg and the crew spied a fully clothed man lying on the iceberg. He could have been asleep but the crew ascertained that he was actually quite dead. It was impossible to reach him so the ship passed him by and allowed his remains to be swallowed by the sea when the iceberg eventually melted.[1]

On March 7, 1861, *Marco Polo* herself struck an iceberg and suffered heavy damage, apparently as the result of the inebriation of the mate on deck (who afterwards spent the next month in irons). Her bowsprit was ripped off, her bow was stove-in and her forward mast was sprung (i.e., rendered unserviceable) and the ship began taking on water. For an entire month, the *Marco Polo's* crew laboured to keep the ship afloat until she made port at Valparaiso, Chile, where the necessary emergency repairs could be made. When the *Marco*

Polo returned to Liverpool in its damaged condition, James Baines, her owner now for ten years, decided that he must forego any further losses and expenses concerning the *Marco Polo*. Baines knew that the softwoods used in Canadian ship construction had a tendency to absorb water, which could slow a ship much more so than the oak and teak ships that British yards produced and that, over time, there would be a marked falling off in the *Marco Polo's* renowned speed. And so Baines decided to sell his famous ship to other shipowners plying the Great Britain – Australia route.

Under her new owners, the *Marco Polo* continued in passenger service to Australia but she no longer flew the flag of the Black Ball Line. By 1867, the year that the separate provinces of British North America entered into a confederation as the new state of Canada, the *Marco Polo* was nearing the end of her career as a passenger vessel.

Older now, and with her timbers saturated with water, the *Marco Polo* could no longer reach the speeds that she routinely displayed in her prime. Nevertheless, she was still capable of surprises. A famous story in her history concerned a passage that the *Marco Polo* made from Australia to Britain in her final year in passenger service. In January 1867, Captain Thomas Labbet RN, of Brisbane, Australia, took passage from Melbourne, Australia, to Britain. He had considered taking the *Marco Polo* but time was of the essence and he calculated that the steamer *Great Britain* was likely to get him to Britain much quicker than the old square-rigger so he booked his passage on the steamship.

Both ships departed Melbourne around the same time. After Captain Labbet was at sea for a week he came up on the deck of the *Great Britain* one day and heard a lookout shout out a report of a sailing vessel lying ahead. The lookout then exclaimed that it was the *Marco Polo*, an assertion that was scoffed at by *Great Britain's* crew. But the lookout, who had once sailed in the *Marco Polo*, knew of what he spake, and he was proven correct when the *Great Britain* closed upon the sailing vessel. The incredulous crew of the *Great Britain*, which had left Melbourne slightly before the *Marco Polo* watched spellbound as their ship passed the *Marco Polo* and then continued steadily on her way. The *Great Britain* ultimately made a very timely passage from Australia to Great Britain.

The *Great Britain* sighted Ireland just around the time that she was scheduled to reach the Hibernian Isle, and picked up a pilot at Cork, Ireland. Sailing through St. George's channel Captain Labbet asked the pilot if he had recently seen or heard anything of note. Nothing in particular the pilot replied, except that he had seen the famous *Marco Polo* — she had passed up St. George's channel eight days previously! One can only imagine Captain Labbet's surprise at hearing that the old clipper ship had beaten his steamship by more than a week!

Perhaps it was her age, or perhaps her current owners skimped on her normal maintenance but for whatever reason later that year the *Marco Polo* failed her passenger vessel inspection, and she was retired from passenger service, returning once again to where she had begun, as a freighter.

[1] See The Wind Commands, at p. 195.

8

Chapter 8. Steam Catches Sail

Through the 1870s and on into the 1880s *Marco Polo* continued to ply the world's oceans. No longer the fast ship that she once was and now old and weakened structurally with water-saturated timbers, she pursued her vocation as a freighter. Her appearance on the horizon often drew the vision of the crews of passing ships, all of whom had heard stories about this legendary greyhound of the seas. She remained a storied ship for her earlier achievements, and many of those who saw her in her later years wondered how long she might continue to ply the high seas.

Marco Polo had lasted longer than many of her contemporaries. The era of the extreme clippers that reached the epitome of square-rigger design under the capable hands of Donald McKay lasted only to the outbreak of the US Civil War in 1861. During the Civil War the US merchant fleet, which was then second-largest in the world, declined by a third and it was slow to recover after the end of the war.

Though the extreme clippers reached the all-time heights of speed achieved by square-rigged ships they cost too much to build and their operating costs were too high, necessitated by the large crews necessary to sail them. For example, the *Sovereign of the Seas* required a crew of 103 to sail the ship. In addition, the narrow hulls of the extreme clippers prevented them from carrying large cargoes. Extreme clippers were pushed hard by their captains' demands for high speeds, thereby straining the integrity of the ships and leading to ripped sails, dislodged spars, and increased pressure on the ship's hulls. The clippers suffered shortened lifespans as a result. Clippers also represented a very specialized ship design and they were very dependent on particular market conditions. The end of the mid-century gold rushes in California, Australasia, and the interior of British Columbia reduced demand for very quick passages at exorbitant fares[1] and lessened the demand for the world's fastest sailing ships. Shipowners adapted by cost-cutting, and by cramming more cargo into the ships' hulls. Labour-saving devices were employed to reduce the need for large crews, albeit sometimes with a slight reduction in average speeds.

Donald McKay's clippers are remembered both for their speed, their physical beauty, and for the poetry of their names. But wooden ships were always susceptible to fire, a significant risk at sea, as well as in port. McKay's *Stag Hound* burned at sea off Pernambuco, Brazil, and the *James Baines* burned at Liverpool, which was a great blow to her namesake, and to his Black Ball Line. The *Great Republic*, McKay's largest clipper and his greatest creation, which was graced by a five-foot-long eagle as a figurehead, burned at her wharf in New York City even before her maiden voyage. Though salvaged, McKay deemed her a wreck and sold her. After repairs, she went to sea in 1853, but weakened by the ordeal that she had suffered the *Great Republic* set no speed records and was not considered to be a successful ship. She was eventually sold to Canadian interests and afterwards sank near Bermuda. McKay's most famous ship, the beautiful *Flying Cloud*, was grounded, wrecked, and ultimately burned as a navigation hazard near St. John, New Brunswick.

Two technological forces now combined to consign square-rigged sailing ships to the history books. The first transformation was the replacement of wooden-hulled ships by ships of iron and steel. The second transformation was the shift from sailing ships to steamships. Although the two transformations were separate, they were related.

At first many thought that a ship made of iron would sink and the public laughed at suggestions that metal could replace wood on the world's oceans. From about 1820 onwards however, the first iron-hulled ships began to appear, and in the 1830s and 1840s iron hulls proved their worth when some of the iron ships that grounded in heavy weather were subsequently refloated and escaped destruction with only minor damage while comparable wooden-hulled ships suffered catastrophic failure when they grounded in heavy seas. All ships built with wooden planks had inherent points of weakness where the planks of the hull were joined together but metal hulls had no such weakness. British inventor and entrepreneur Isambard Kingdom Brunel constructed the iron-hulled *Great Britain* in 1843 (a ship that still exists in 2025) which proved the seaworthiness of iron-hulled ships.

For a time, particularly in Great Britain, the designers of clipper ships sought to improve the strength of wooden ships by building them with an iron frame and then planking that iron frame with wood. Those so-called composite clippers became the last word in clipper design. (In the twenty-first century one of those ships, the British clipper *Cutty Sark*, the last survivor from the age of the clipper ships, is a fine example of a composite clipper.)

Steam power, which began to be employed in the earlier years of the nineteenth century steadily progressed as the century proceeded. The steamship, slow but steady, eventually outclassed the great clipper ships as the greyhounds of the sea. The advantages of steamships were multiple. They provided more cargo-carrying capacity than the clippers and thus freight and passenger costs per unit were reduced. Steamships provided steady progress regardless of the weather and were therefore more able to maintain average speeds and regular sailing schedules, which was an important factor as transportation and communication developments brought the far corners of the world closer together. Over time the improvements in steam propulsion technology resulted in the steamships outclassing the great wind ships even in maximum speeds.

The year 1869 was pivotal in the transformation of marine transportation as a result of two significant events. On May 10, 1869, a transcontinental railway was completed across the North American continent with the hammering of a golden spike into the last rail in the Utah Territory. The completion of an American transcontinental railway had been delayed by the US Civil War but its post-war completion now permitted a much quicker and safer method of transportation between the east and west coasts of North America. No longer would it be necessary for passengers, or time-sensitive freight, to negotiate the harsh passage around Cape Horn to reach California and other points on the West coast of North America. By 1900, there would be four more transcontinental railways built in the United States, and, in 1885, a transcontinental railway would span Canada in the form of the Canadian Pacific Railway. The completion of transcontinental railways in North America ended the need for fast sailing ships to move people and cargo around South America to reach the western side of the North American continent.

The other transformational event in 1869 occurred on November 16, 1869, in Egypt. As the sun shone down on the town of Port Said along the Egyptian shoreline some 80 vessels crowded into the man-made harbour, all gaily decorated with bright pennants to bear witness to a mighty historical event — the opening of the Suez Canal. A French-led effort directed by Ferdinand de Lesseps had succeeded in breaching the barrier between the Mediterranean Sea and the Red Sea despite many obstacles. Now princes and potentates were present as de Lessep's vision came to fruition. On board the warships and merchant craft in the harbour were the Emperor of Austria-Hungary, the Crown Prince of Prussia, a prince of the Netherlands, and many ambassadors, admirals, and generals from many countries. Canons boomed out salutes to the Egyptian ruler, the Khedive, and to his suzerain, the Ottoman Sultan. Then, as the smoke of the cannon salutes dissipated, the graceful French Imperial yacht *Aigle* sailed forth with the elegant French Empress Eugénie present as the guest of honour. In the afternoon the assembled dignitaries gathered in the desert to worship according to Christian and Moslem rites, followed by nighttime fireworks. The following day, led by the *Agile* the ships entered the canal and proceeded over the following three days to transit the canal to its southern port of Suez, with stopovers along the way for formal balls and more fireworks.

The Suez Canal reduced sea voyages to the Orient, India, and Australasia by thousands of kilometres. No longer would ships from European ports have to make the long trek around the Cape of Good Hope to reach the far side of the world. And the Suez Canal was tailor-made for iron-hulled steamships which could traverse the canal at a steady speed and navigate the reef-strewn Red Sea without mishaps. With the opening of the Suez Canal, a steamship could sail from Europe to Asia in only three weeks.

Although Great Britain was initially opposed to the canal because of Britain's traditional rivalry with France the British were actually well positioned to take advantage of the canal as a result of the transformation in marine transportation that was occurring with the switch to steam-driven and iron-hulled ships. Britain's lead over other countries in industrial technology allowed it to capture a great deal of worldwide shipbuilding and, in the 1880s and 1890s, the shipyards in Glasgow were the most productive in the world. Britain also profited from its stable politics, its resources in both coal and iron, and its good domestic communications that easily brought together financiers, shipping lines, and shipbuilding firms.

Throughout those years Samuel Cunard's company continued to gain a stellar reputation for speed, comfort, and safety in transatlantic operations. Cunard counselled his ship masters to maintain caution and reliability and the statistics illustrate the strong adherence of Cunard's masters to those standards. For the first 75 years of the Cunard Line, there were no fatalities on a Cunard ship due to a shipwreck, and for the first 35 years, there was no loss of life from any misadventure on a Cunard vessel. That contrasted well with the experience of other shipping lines, which often suffered disasters and losses that undermined public confidence in their ships. The American author Mark Twain remarked that even the biblical Noah would have had to work his way up the ranks from the bottom if he had been employed by the Cunard Line! Canadians and Americans flocked to the Cunard Line, and its success was assured by its reputation.

Samuel Cunard long maintained that his company's transatlantic fleet should be designed as paddle wheel steamships but he was eventually persuaded that a screw propulsion system might serve the company better. The last Cunard paddle wheeler launched was the attractive *Scotia* in 1862, the fastest ship of its day on the North Atlantic runs. She was followed by the first Cunard screw propulsion ship, the *China*, which proved the cost savings inherent in the more efficient screw propulsion system. The *China* was followed by the *Cuba*, which was also designed with a propeller system. Faced with the proven success of propellers over paddles the Cunard line never built another paddle steamer after launching the ever-popular *Scotia*.

An old man now, Samuel Cunard's time was passing. In declining health, he retired from commerce in 1863 and made a last, nostalgic trip to Halifax, the city of his birth in 1864. Returning to England, he lived his remaining time in Kensington, in London, England. Created a baronet by Queen Victoria, and therefore now knighted as Sir Samuel Cunard, Bart., he slowly faded away in the early months of 1865, and on April 28, 1865, he died at the age of 77. In his later years, he harkened back to the beginning of the great shipping firm that now bore his name and said of it: "I originated this service at a great risk and at a time when no other party could be found to undertake it . . . [resulting in] a beautiful line of communication between the eastern and western world."[2] Cunard left behind a shipping business that continued the advancement of steam over sail and of iron and steel over wood. Between 1870 and 1890 that transformation was essentially completed.

By 1870 the American extreme clippers were gone although the British tea clippers, smaller ships such as *Ariel*, *Taeping*, and *Cutty Sark*, lasted longer by hauling tea from the Orient to Britain. Races between the tea clippers to see which ship would be first to land its precious cargo of tea were closely watched by the public in Britain and they lent romance to the last days of the clippers. But the opening of the Suez Canal impacted the economic viability of the tea clippers as did the opening of the Canadian Pacific Railway in 1885, which allowed ships to drop cargoes at Vancouver, British Columbia, for carriage east by the Canadian Pacific Railway to Montreal for onward passage by sea to Liverpool, resulting in an overall saving in the total time tea cargoes spent in transit from the Orient.

In the mid-1850s, after the burning and sinking of the *Great Republic*, Donald McKay no longer built the beautiful extreme clippers with whom his name is most closely associated. Rather, bowing to market conditions and financial imperatives, he began building more medium clippers. A financial crisis in 1857 over the ownership shares of British ships in which McKay had an interest led to the temporary closing of his shipyard but he quickly rebounded in no small part due to the support he received from Enoch Train, one of his prime American customers who was also one of his creditors. Train persuaded McKay's other creditors not to force McKay out of business but to allow his work to continue to clear his debts.

The outbreak of the Civil War following the secession of South Carolina in 1860 dealt a heavy blow to American merchant shipping because of the heavy depredations on the US merchant marine by Confederate raiders such as the *CSS Alabama*, and the *CSS Shenandoah*, which caused US marine insurance rates to skyrocket. Many US businesses turned to British and other foreign-flagged vessels to avoid the exorbitant costs of marine transportation during those years. American shipping firms also re-flagged their vessels as foreign ships to avoid being confronted at sea by the Confederate Navy. Donald McKay adapted by equipping his shipyard to build iron ships and both marine and locomotive engines. During the war, McKay built four small steamships for the Union Navy but he incurred significant financial costs in doing so because of US Navy design changes. It would subsequently take McKay and his family many years to obtain partial compensation from the US government for the extraordinary expenses that resulted from those design changes.

After the war, the US merchant shipping business did not recover and McKay's yard built mostly smaller ships, such as schooners and sloops. Despite his international fame as a naval architect, and as a shipbuilder, financial success always eluded Donald McKay. Nevertheless, McKay never lost his passion for the great Clippers. In a letter to his brother, he described his ships as "monuments on the ocean" that "float triumphantly on every sea."[3]

Exceptionally, McKay's last extreme clipper was built after the war and for his own account — the *Glory of the Seas*, which was launched in 1869, the year that world shipping was transformed by the opening of the transcontinental railway and the Suez Canal. That same year McKay lost the *Glory of the Seas* to his creditors after he sailed aboard her around Cape Horn and into San Francisco harbour where he received a telegraph advising him that his creditors had seized his ship.[4] The following year McKay narrowly escaped another insolvency crisis as his business continued to decline. His last effort was a fitting one — he undertook the overhaul and re-rigging of the famous schooner yacht *America* for which the America's Cup trophy is named, and which is still awarded in the twenty-first century for the fastest speeds attained by competing sailing yachts.

Aging now, and with the great years of his windships behind him McKay closed his yard in 1875 and retired to a farm near Hamilton, Massachusetts. That same year, his most beautiful creation, the *Flying Cloud*, met her end at the birthplace of the Marco Polo in St. John, New Brunswick, where the *Flying Cloud* was wrecked and then burned on a sandbar after trying unsuccessfully to reach sanctuary in port when a terrible storm turned her back from a voyage to Europe. Donald McKay survived his most famous ship by only five years, dying at the age of 70 on September 20, 1880, after suffering a stroke. His legacy lies in the remembered beauty and speed of the great windships that he designed and built.

James Baines, the British shipowner who played such an outsized role in mid-century shipping through the *Marco Polo*, and his orders for clippers built by Donald McKay, continued in the shipping trade for some years. By 1860, the Black Ball Line possessed 86 vessels and employed 3300 officers and seamen. But Baines suffered a heavy blow in 1858 when the *James Baines*, one of the four extreme clippers that he had ordered from Donald McKay, burned at Liverpool. He remained successful into the 1860s but he probably remained in wooden sailing ships too long because his fleet began to eat up his profits in repairs, and the steamships he competed with increasingly offered more flexibility in marine operations. Baines did take financial interests in two of the most famous steamships of the era, the *Great Britain* and the *Great Eastern*, but neither investment was lucrative for him. Then, in 1863, his reputation suffered damage when Baines was caught up in a stock manipulation scandal and a few years later, in 1866, he was hit very hard by the failure of Barneds Bank, necessitating the sale of some two-thirds of the Black Ball Line's fleet. Baines tried to recoup his misfortunes with a move into steamships but in 1871 the Black Ball Line failed.

James Baines eventually died in straitened circumstances at the age of 66 in 1889.

James Nicol (Bully) Forbes, the favourite captain of James Baines and the remarkable master of the Marco Polo went on to command the *Lightning*, one of the clipper ships that James Baines had ordered from the shipyard of Donald McKay in East Boston. In her, Forbes made famous passages, though perhaps none that approached his epic-making voyages in command of the Marco Polo. Given command of the Scottish-built clipper ship *Schomberg*, Forbes suffered a mishap when the ship was caught in an uncharted current while coming into Melbourne and thrust onto an uncharted sandbar where she was wrecked. Although all of the passengers and crew were saved and her cargo was salvaged before the *Schomberg* broke up in heavy seas, Forbes seemed to be deeply affected by the experience. An official inquiry found Forbes to be blameless for the loss of the *Schomberg* but Forbes never recovered from the blow of losing his ship. He subsequently drifted in and out of lesser commands before taking early retirement from the sea. He retired to a residence overlooking the Mersey River where he died on June 4, 1874, at the age of 54. The memory of his triumph as master of the *Marco Polo* was recalled on his tombstone, upon which was inscribed the words: "James Nicol Forbes, Master of the Famous Marco Polo."[5]

James Smith, the New Brunswicker who designed and built the *Marco Polo* as his greatest achievement, found himself all at sea in a gale of bad luck following the *Marco Polo*. One of his ships, the *Unicorn*, foundered at sea in 1851, and marine insurance rates on some of his other ships were increased by Lloyds of London owing to the use of resinous woods in their construction. Subsequently, another ship he built was badly damaged on launching, and in a final stroke, his shipyard caught fire on April 28, 1855, burning a ship under construction and various stores, leaving Smith with large losses. Smith built only one other ship after that event. James Smith passed away in Woodstock New Brunswick in 1876, at the age of 73. Despite his reverses in later years his conception, design, and construction of the *Marco Polo* enhanced the reputation of Canadian shipbuilders and helped to spark a demand for Canadian ships that resulted in years of prosperity for Atlantic Canada.

[1] During the California gold rush passenger fares from New York to San Francisco reached as high as $1000.00, equivalent to $40,000.00 in 2025.

[2] Quoted in Transatlantic at p. XVIII.

[3] Quoted in Barons of the Sea, at p. 292.

[4] The Glory of the Seas would survive in the 20th century and would be burned for her metal fittings in 1923.

[5] Quoted in The Saltwater Men, at p. 51.

9

Chapter 9. The Final Years

As steam slowly strangled the market for the great windships in the latter part of the nineteenth century, the *Marco Polo* carried on. She remained a legendary ship on the high seas and was sometimes spoken of in awe by mariners. Now reduced to cargo service like so many other square riggers she went from port to port taking on and delivering guano, coal, or lumber.

A famous tale is told of the *Marco Polo* from those years. Apparently, on a quiet Sunday night, the ship's mate got it into his head to try and catch a shark that had been following the ship. He rigged a large hook with a piece of meat as bait and threw it over the side, with the connivance of the deck crew. Sure enough, the hungry shark took the bait and after playing it out on the line for a time the crew hoisted a 16-foot shark aboard, now exhausted by its exertions. Once on deck, however, the line holding it parted and the shark hit the deck and exploded back to life, thrashing and gnashing as the crew tried desperately to subdue it with clubs. The desperate shark broke through a skylight transom and fell into a cabin below, thoroughly wrecking it with its wild exertions. The deck crew finally succeeded in terminating the giant fish amidst a scene of blood-soaked carnage in the now-wrecked cabin. One can only imagine the reaction of the ship's captain when he surveyed that scene!

During those years *Marco Polo* passed through a succession of British owners from James Baines and Co. to Wilson and Blair, and then Bell and Lawes. The *Marco Polo* carried cargoes for them to and from South America and Europe as well as to the Mediterranean ports, sometimes reaching as far east as the port of Aden on the shores of the Indian Ocean. Efforts were continually made to keep the ship going as she aged. In 1874, her rigging was reduced from a medium clipper rig to a barque with a shortening of her lower yards by some 12 feet. At some point during those years her wooden mainmast was replaced by an iron mast.

By the 1880s the *Marco Polo* was practically clapped out, now taking twice as long to cross the North Atlantic as she had in her heyday as a newly built lumber drogher. Her hull began to deteriorate badly and to maintain her structural integrity her owners wrapped chains around the hull, and installed a pumping system using a windmill to power the pump to deal with an increase of seawater entering the hull. Her British owners finally decided that they could no longer make a profit from her and in 1882 they sold the ship to Captain P. A. Bull from Christiana, Norway. Somehow, in the late days of sail, the Norwegians were still able to generate profits from sailing ships. Her new owner used the *Marco Polo* in lumber service. She was slightly damaged by a fire in 1882, while in port at Quebec City but no real harm was done.

As the *Marco Polo*, now old and frail, made slow passages across the Atlantic old timers among the crews of passing ships took special note of her, and each time they spied her many of them thought and said that this would probably be the last time they would see the famous *Marco Polo*. She came across the Atlantic and home to Canada in the summer of 1883, and took on a cargo of lumber at Montmorency, Quebec. Then she sailed for Europe but this voyage was to be her last. As she left the St Lawrence River and entered the Gulf of St. Lawrence the North Atlantic waves began to press on her from all sides. Her rotten hull began taking on water when one of the chains wrapped around her broke. Her pumps still worked but they could no longer hold back the seas entering her hull. *Marco Polo's* time had come. Her Norwegian master did the only thing that he could do, he pointed the *Marco Polo* towards the nearest shore to run her aground and he ordered that all sails be set, even though he understood that the resulting forward pressure would simply force more water into her hull. But there was nothing else to be done and her crew needed to be saved. In *The Salt-Water Men* historian Joseph Schull considered it "the act of a seaman."[1]

Onshore at Cavendish, Prince Edward Island, the residents were astonished to see a square-rigged ship with all sails set inbound for the shore of the islands. Certainly, they thought that the master must perceive the immediate danger facing his ship. But onward she came.

A visitor from St. John, New Brunswick was surprised by the sight of the ship and he was able to positively identify her to onlookers as the *Marco Polo* because he had supplied some of the materials used in her construction 32 years previously.

By chance, in Cavendish on that day there was an eight-year-old schoolgirl who, as an adult, would win worldwide literary fame as the author of *Anne of Green Gables*, the most popular work of Canadian fiction. She was Lucy Maud Montgomery and although she did not actually witness what happened that day she did hear the great crash that accompanied the beaching and dismasting of the *Marco Polo* on the shores of Prince Edward Island. Later, as a young woman of fifteen, she submitted an essay about the loss of the *Marco Polo* for a competition sponsored by a Montreal newspaper, the *Montreal Daily Witness*, which published Montgomery's account of the wreck of the *Marco Polo* on March 5, 1891.[2] Her account is perhaps the most comprehensive and colourful account of the beaching from those who lived nearby and knew the tale.

THE WIND AND THE SAILS

Lucy Maud Montgomery's account of the wreck deserves recollection here. Her description of the event is as follows:

"What a day that 25th of July was in Cavendish! The wind blew a hurricane and the waves ran mountains high; the storm had begun two days before and had now reached its highest pitch of fury. When at its worst, the report was spread that a large vessel was coming ashore off a little fishing station called Cawnpore, and soon an excited crowd was assembled on the beach. The wind was nor'-nor'-east, as sailors say, and the vessel, coming in before the gale, with every stitch of canvas set, was a sight never to be forgotten! She grounded about 300yards from the shore, and, just as she struck, the crew cut the rigging, and the foremast and the huge iron mainmast, carrying the mizzen-topmast with it, went over with a crash that could be heard for miles above the roaring of the storm! Then the ship broached to and lay there with the waves breaking over her. By this time, half the people in Cavendish were assembled on the beach and the excitement was intense. As long as the crew remained on the vessel they were safe, but, if ignorant of the danger of such a proceeding, they attempted to land, death was certain. When it was seen that they were evidently preparing to hazard a landing all sorts of devices to warn them back were tried, but none were successful until a large board was put up, with the words, "stick to the ship at all hazards" painted on it. When they saw this they made no further attempt to land and thus night fell.

The storm continued all night but by morning was sufficiently abated to permit a boat to go out to the ship and bring the crew ashore. They were a hard-looking lot — tired, wet and hungry, but in high spirits over their rescue, and, while they were refreshing the inner man, the jokes flew thick and fast. One little fellow, on being asked, "if it wasn't pretty windy out there," responded, with a shrug of his shoulders, "Oh, no, dear vas not too mooch vind but der vas too mooch vater!"

Lively times for Cavendish followed. The crew, consisting of about twenty men, found boarding places around the settlement and contrived to keep the neighborhood in perpetual uproar, while the fussy good-natured captain came to our place. He was a corpulent, bustling little man, bluff and hearty – the typical sea-captain; he was idolized by his crew, who would have gone through fire and water for him any day. And such a crew! Almost every nationality was represented. There were Norwegians, Swedes, Dutchmen, Englishmen, Irishmen, Spaniards, two Tahitians, and one quarrelsome, obstinate little German who refused to work his passage home and demanded to be sent back to his fatherland by steamer. it was amusing to hear them trying to master the pronunciation of our English names. We had a dog called "Gyp" whose name was a constant source of vexation to them. The Norwegians called him "Yip," the irritable little German termed him "schnip" and one old tar twisted it into "ship."

But the time passed all too quickly by. The "Marco Polo" and her cargo were sold to parties in St. John, N.B., and the captain and his motley crew took their departure. A company of men were at once hired to assist in taking out her cargo and eighteen schooner loads of deal [i.e. planking] were taken from her. The planks had so swelled from the wet that it was found necessary to cut her beams through in order to get them out and consequently she was soon nothing but a mere shell with about half of her cargo still in her."[3]

Montgomery also described how a salvage crew made the

mistake of overnighting on the wreck about a month after the *Marco Polo* came ashore and during that night the sea rose and a great storm endangered their lives. One abortive attempt to escape from the wreck resulted in the death of one man after which the others held on for dear life. The savagery of the storm broke the wreck apart but fortunately, the salvage crew was able to remain on the ship's forecastle, which remained above water until the storm subsided sufficiently to allow for a successful rescue attempt by rescuers on shore. All of the remaining members of the salvage crew were saved. A salvage sale was held shortly afterwards netting 5500 pounds sterling for the cargo, and 600 pounds sterling for the remains of the ship.

About one month later another storm washed away the final remains of the ship. So ended the *Marco Polo*, Canada's most famous square-rigged sailing vessel. Not for her a burning, or consignment to some wrecker's yard. She came ashore in Canada, the land of her birth, with her cloud of sails proudly flying one final time as she reached for her homeland's shore.

[1] Schull, The Saltwater Men, at page 144.

[2] Montgomery's account was also published in the Charlottetown Daily Patriot on March 11, 1891.

[3] Quoted in Hollenberg, Marco Polo, at pp. 117-18 and Dokumen, A Name for Herself, at pp. 7-8.

The Wind And The Sails

Epilogue: Remembrance

The nineteenth century was an era of ferment and technological change in the shipping industry. Rapid technological progress and a public demand for better transportation and communications with the remote parts of the world led to the greatest achievements in sailing ship design, and then the replacement of wood and sail by iron and steam. Canadians played outsized roles in the transformation of the shipping industry in the nineteenth century, giving to America Donald McKay, its greatest sailing ship designer, and builder, and giving to Great Britain an entrepreneur, Sir Samuel Cunard, Bart., who created Britain's preeminent passenger steamship company.

By comparison, James Smith of St. John New Brunswick was perhaps not in the same league as either McKay or Cunard as a transformational historical figure in the shipbuilding and shipping industry but he did create in Canada a ship that became a legend for its speed and that ship, the *Marco Polo*, created an international appreciation of Canadian shipbuilding that would help to transform the economy of the maritime provinces during the middle years of the nineteenth century. Deservedly, he should be remembered for his masterpiece of shipbuilding, the *Marco Polo*.

The *Marco Polo* was the greatest of all the square-rigged ships built in Canada in the nineteenth century. Whether the cause of her fame was her design by James Smith, the business foresight of James Baines who purchased her, or the knowledge and skill of her great master James Nicol Forbes, *Marco Polo* was undoubtedly the sensation of her times within the British Empire in the middle years of the nineteenth century.

Perhaps her fame was a combination of many factors. Certainly, James Smith designed and built a vessel that was much different in conception and scale from the vessels hitherto designed and built in New Brunswick. The misfortunes of her near wreck while on the stocks, and of her botched launch certainly left *Marco Polo* an imperfect creation and created a myth, generally unsupported by the principles of naval architecture, that her distended keel created some kind of sea witchery that accounted for her speed. But beyond all question, *Marco Polo* was well-served by her famous commander, James Nicol Forbes. His natural skills as a seaman, and as a navigator, were on display when he used the great circle routes and the wind and current charts of Matthew Fontain Maury to blaze a new marine path to the southern continent. The combination of a great ship, and a great master, made the world a smaller place in the mid-nineteenth century and hastened the development of the connections between continents and countries that are taken for granted today.

The remains of the *Marco Polo* now lie off of the shores of Prince Edward Island National Park, and the ship's grave is a National Historic Site, which seeks to integrate the story of the *Marco Polo* into the narrative of the park. At her birthplace in St. John, New Brunswick, the *Marco Polo* is also well remembered at the provincial museum located in St. John. A bridge that crosses Marsh Creek where she was built is fittingly named the Marco Polo Bridge. A short film on the subject of the Marco Polo has been produced by the National Film Board of Canada and her image has also graced a special commemorative coin issued by the Royal Canadian Mint, as well as a special commemorative stamp issued by Canada Post. A special commemorative stamp showcasing the Marco Polo has also been issued by Australia Post.

The story of the *Marco Polo* is one part of a larger story of how Canadians participated in, and rose to prominence, in the maritime trade of the nineteenth century. For a time after confederation in 1867, the total tonnage of vessels registered in Canada made Canada the fourth largest shipping country in the world. But as iron and steam eventually triumphed over wood and sail the shipyards in the maritime provinces found it difficult to compete and the Canadian merchant marine withered. After 1890, Canadian shipyards no longer built square-rigged ships, and an era in Canadian history passed.[1] By 1910 the size of the Canadian merchant fleet had been surpassed by nine other countries.

Although sail lingered on for a time on the world's shipping routes, finding cargoes of guano, coal, Australian wool, and grain they had to drop their shipping charges and often barely eked out a living. The clipper ship by then had given way to the last evolution of sail in the form of the Down-Easter, a square-rigger with a hull filled out to maximize cargo capacity, without the highest sails, the moonrakers, and without studding sails. Built with oak frames that were strengthened by iron strapping, copper sheathing, and yellow pine for planking they plied the seas for a short while but they could not compete effectively with the new steel steamships.

The very last iteration of sail came from Germany, in the form of the all-steel *Preussen* of 1902 with a steel hull and five steel masts that could deploy 60,000 square feet of sail and drive her at 17 knots. Sadly, *Preussen* herself was rammed and wrecked by a steamship in the English Channel that had attempted to cross her bows and misjudged the two ships' relative speeds. The final blows that extinguished sailing ships came with the opening of the Panama Canal in 1914, and the outbreak of the Great War in the same year. Sailing ships made easy prey for German raiders and U-boats and many of them were lost before the war came to an end. Today, except for some school ships, the great square-riggers are but a memory as reflected in this east coast sea chantey epitaph:

The Wind And The Sails

"I'd like to ship off-shore again upon some Bluenose barque,

And shout a sailor chantey in the windy, starry dark,

Or fist a dewed-up tops'l in a black south-easter's roar

But it ain't no use a-wishin, for them days will come no more." [2]

[1] Exceptionally, the historian Thomas H. Raddall noted in the Forward to Archibald MacMechan's Tales of the Sea that the last square-rigged ship built in Canada was the barquentine Maid of England that was launched at Grosse Coques, Nova Scotia, in 1920, long after the heyday of sail.

[2] Quoted in Illustrated History, at p. 369.

THE WIND AND THE SAILS

Appendix: Who was Marco Polo?

Marco Polo was a Venetian merchant and travel writer who opened the eyes of Europeans to the civilizations and cultures of the Eurasian landmass east of Constantinople in the thirteenth century. Born in Venice around 1254, he travelled with his uncles over the Silk Road to fabulous Cathay beginning in 1269. Eventually, he would produce a book of his travels that described the world from the Polar Seas in the north to the island of Java in the south, from Japan in the east to Zanzibar in the west, and many points in between. Some of the places that Marco Polo visited in the late 1200s were not visited by Europeans again for another 600 years – until the opening of the Burma Road in World War Two.

Marco Polo's travels were enabled by the sudden rise of the Tartar Empire in the Orient. Beginning around the year 1206 the Mongol peoples under Genghis Khan embarked upon wide-scale conquest in the east. Within twelve years they had conquered northern China, which they called Cathay, and, in the following forty years, they swept across

Eurasia seizing all lands except Indochina, India, Arabia, and western Europe. Soon after they organized their empire with the eastern portion of Cathay and Manzi under the direct rule of the Great Khan while the western territories were placed under Khans who were subordinate to the Great Khan. For a brief period, this vast empire afforded protection to travellers who embarked upon the long overland journey from Europe to the Orient.

In 1260, two Venetian merchant brothers Niccolo and Maffeo Polo journeyed east to Constantinople and then onwards to Sudak, a Venetian colony in the Crimea, where they met up with a third brother, Marco the Elder. The three then set off to the east and journeyed to the court of the Great Khan, now Kublai Khan, a descendant of Genghis Khan who had been Sinicized although retaining some aspects of his family's nomadic past. Kublai Khan was a combination of the simple nomad and the cultured Chinese noble embodying the compassionate spirit of Buddhism. He was also a man of much energy and competence who reinvigorated and masterfully controlled the governments of his domain.

Curious about the civilization in the west he sent the Polo brothers back to Europe on a mission to the Pope. When it came time to return to Cathay the brothers took along with them the young Marco Polo, now aged seventeen. Marco Polo journeyed with his uncles across the Eurasian landmass along the Silk Road from Palestine to Peking where the Great Khan was impressed by the young Marco Polo's intelligence and modesty. Marco became a favourite of the Great Khan and was appointed as a foreign emissary. As such, Marco Polo was engaged in many travels on behalf of Kublai Khan to Burma, India, Indochina, the East Indies, and Ceylon. He also wrote about places farther afield, including Abyssinia, Zanzibar, and Madagascar, where he related the legendary stories about the mythical Rukhs, a bird of vast size that was said to be capable of lifting an elephant, and which Polo ascribed to the mythical European gryphon.

After nearly twenty years in the service of the Great Khan Marco Polo and his uncles Niccolo and Maffeo returned to Europe in 1292 travelling through the Malay Straits as special emissaries of Kublai Khan escorting a princess bride for Arghun, the Tartar Khan of the Levant in Persia. After completing their mission the Polos returned home to Venice, arriving there in 1295, where they had been gone for so long that their family did not at first recognize them, believing them to have perished!

In his later years, Marco Polo served as a soldier in a war on the Italian peninsula that resulted in his becoming a prisoner of war in Genoa in 1298. In captivity, Marco Polo began to recount the stories of his travels to a fellow prisoner, one Rustichello of Pisa, a romance writer who became Marco Polo's ghostwriter for his travel memoir. The result was a book now known as *The Travels of Marco Polo* which captures an observant Marco Polo's eye for the appearance and customs of the many different peoples he encountered including the

Chinese, Tartars, Tibetans, Turks, Persians, Indians, and others. Polo also had a good eye for the flora and fauna of the places he went to and he described many of the plants and birds he encountered quite accurately. His account remains a classic of travel literature in the twenty-first century.

Marco Polo died in Venice in 1324.

Image Credits

Cover and Frontispiece – *Marco Polo*, painted by Thomas Robertson, 1859, courtesy State Library of Victoria (Australia), public domain

Page 17 – *Flying Cloud*, courtesy Wikimedia Commons, public domain

Page 19 – Donald McKay, by Southwark and Hawes, circa 1850-55, courtesy Wikimedia Commons, public domain

Page 26 – *Royal William*, by the Post Office Department (Canada) 1933, courtesy Wikimedia Commons, public domain

Page 31 – Sir Samuel Cunard, Bart., painter unknown, courtesy Wikimedia Commons (from the Nova Scotia Archives), public domain

Page 41 – The *Marco Polo* under sail, Courtesy Wikimedia

Commons (from the State Library of Queensland (Australia) no. 1 112300 Marco Polo (ship).jpg), public domain

Page 70 – The *Marco Polo* at port in Australia, Courtesy Wikimedia Commons (from the State Library of Queensland (Australia) no. 1 144587 Marco Polo (ship).jpg), public domain

Bibliography

Brown, Craig (ed.), *The Illustrated History of Canada*, Key Porter Books, Toronto, 2007

De Villiers, Marq, *Witch in the Wind; True Story of the Legendary Bluenose*, Thomas Allen Publishers, Toronto, 2007

Durnford, Hugh (ed.), *Heritage of Canada; Our Storied Past and Where to Find It*, Readers Digest Association of Canada, Montreal, 1978

Fox, Stephen, *Transatlantic; Samuel Cunard, Isambard Brunel, and the Great Atlantic Steamships*, Perennial/Harper Collins, New York, 2004

Hardy, W. G., (Costain, Thomas, ed.), *From Sea to Sea: The Road to Nationhood 1850-1910* (Volume 4 of The Canadian History Series), Doubleday & Company, Garden City (New York), 1959

Hollenberg, Martin J., *Marco Polo; The Story of the Fastest Clipper*, Nimbus Publishing, Halifax (Nova Scotia), 2006

Jones, Eric C (Capt.) and Nolan, Christopher D. (Lt.), *Eagle Seamanship; A Manual for Square-Rigger Sailing*, Naval Institute Press, Annapolis (Maryland), 2011

Judson, Clara Ingram, *Yankee Clippers; The Story of Donald McKay*, Follett Publishing Company, Chicago, 1965

Langley, John G., *Steam Lion; A Biography of Samuel Cunard*, Brick Tower Press, Shelter Island Heights (New York), 2008

Lavery, Brian, *Ship; The Epic Story of Maritime Adventure*, Smithsonian Institution - National Maritime Museum - DK Publishing, New York, 2004

Lewis, Edward V. and O'Brien, Robert, *Ships*, Time-Life Books, New York, 1965

Lubbock, Basil, *The Colonial Clippers, Second Edition*, James Brown & Son (Project Gutenberg e-book 2016), Glasgow, 1921

MacMechan, Archibald (Forward by Thomas H. Raddall), *Tales of the Sea*, McClelland & Stewart, Toronto, 1947

Maxtone-Graham, John, *The Only Way to Cross*, Collier Books, New York, 1972

Miles, Vincent J., *Transatlantic Train: The Untold Story of the Boston Merchant Who Launched Donald McKay to Fame*, Dorchester Historical Society, Dorchester (Mass.) 2022

Morton, Harry, (Drawings by Don Hermansen and Paul Dwillies - original drawings by Peggy Morton), *The Wind Commands;*

Sailors and Sailing Ships in the Pacific, Wesleyan University Press, Middletown (Conn.) & UBC Press, Vancouver, 1975

Osterhammel, Jurgen (translated by Patrick Camiller), *The Transformation of the World; A Global History of the Nineteenth Century*, Princeton University Press, Princeton and Oxford, 2014

Polo, Marco, (translated by Ronald Latham), *The Travels of Marco Polo*, The Folio Society, London, 1968

Sager, Eric W., and Fischer, Lewis R., *Shipping and Shipbuilding in Atlantic Canada 1820-1914*, Canadian Historical Association (Historical Booklet N. 42), Ottawa, 1986

Schull, Joseph, (illustrations by Ed McNally), *The Salt-Water Men; Canada's Deep-Sea Sailors*, MacMillan, Toronto, 1960

Ujifusa, Steven, *Barons of the Sea; And their Race to Build the World's Fastest Clipper Ship*, Simon & Schuster, New York, 2018

Villiers, Alan (Capt.), *Men Ships and the Sea*, National Geographic Society, Washington (D.C.), 1962

Villiers, Alan (Capt.), *Men Ships and the Sea (New Edition)*, National Geographic Society, Washington (D.C.), 1973

Wallace, Frederick William, *Wooden Ships and Iron Men: The Story of the Square-Rigged Merchant Marine of British North America, the Ships, their Builders and Owners, and the Men Who Sailed Them*, Hodder and Stoughton Ltd., London (England) and Toronto, 1924

Wallace, Frederick William, *In the Wake of the Wind-Ships; notes, records and biographies pertaining to the square-rigged merchant marine of British North America*, G. Sully and Company, New York, 1927

Wilson, Garth, *A History of Shipbuilding and Naval Architecture in Canada*, National Museum of Science and Technology, Ottawa, 1994 https://publications.gc.ca/collections/collection_2018/mstc-cstm/NM97-2-1-4-eng.pdf

www.ingramcontent.com/pod-product-compliance
Lightning Source LLC
Chambersburg PA
CBHW060617080526
44585CB00013B/874